HOME PLANNERS
OUTDOOR
PROJECT
COLLECTION

113 EASY-TO-BUILD PROJECTS

HOME PLANNERS
OUTDOOR
PROJECT
C O L L E C T I O N

Published by Home Planners, LLC
Wholly owned by Hanley-Wood, LLC

President, Jayne Fenton
Chief Financial Officer, Joe Carroll
Vice President, Publishing, Jennifer Pearce
Vice President, Retail Sales, Chuck Tripp
Vice President, General Manager, Marc Wheeler
Executive Editor, Linda Bellamy
National Sales Manager, Book Division, Julie Marshall
Managing Editor, Jason D. Vaughan
Special Projects Editor, Kristin Schneidler
Associate Editors, Nate Ewell, Kathryn R. Sears
Lead Plans Associate, Morenci C. Clark
Plans Associates, Jill M. Hall, Elizabeth Landry, Nick Nieskes
Proofreaders/Copywriters, Douglas Jenness, Sarah Lyons
Technical Specialist, Jay C. Walsh
Lead Data Coordinator, Fran Altemose
Data Coordinators, Misty Boler, Melissa Siewert
Production Director, Sara Lisa
Production Manager, Brenda McClary

Big Designs, Inc.
President, Creative Director, Anthony D'Elia
Vice President, Business Manager, Megan D'Elia
Vice President, Design Director, Chris Bonavita
Editorial Director, John Roach
Assistant Editor, Tricia Starkey
Director of Design and Production, Stephen Reinfurt
Group Art Director, Kevin Limongelli
Photo Editor, Christine DiVuolo
Managing Art Director, Jessica Hagenbuch
Graphic Designer, Mary Ellen Mulshine
Graphic Designer, Lindsey O'Neill-Myers
Graphic Designer, Jacque Young
Assistant Photo Editor, Brian Wilson
Project Director, David Barbella
Assistant Production Manager, Rich Fuentes

Photo Credits

Front Cover and Title Page:
Photography by Mark Lohman

Back Cover:
Photo: © 2001 Getty Images

Home Planners Corporate Headquarters
3275 W. Ina Road, Suite 220
Tucson, Arizona 85741

Distribution Center
29333 Lorie Lane
Wixom, Michigan 48393

© 2003

10 9 8 7 6 5 4 3 2 1

Printed in the United States of America

Library of Congress Catalog Control Number: 2003113854

ISBN: 1-931131-22-8

HOME PLANNERS
OUTDOOR
PROJECT
COLLECTION

FEATURE

PROJECTS

ORDER INFORMATION

A romantic gazebo, such as the one shown here, adds a special flair to any yard. For more information, see page 21.

Building Basics For Outdoor Projects

Imagine a playhouse for your children just outside your kitchen window; or your very own shed for gardening or craft tools; or a lovely garden swing nestled in a secluded, shady area by the side of your home. Perhaps, instead, your yard would benefit from a pool cabana or a bridge over a rocky or marshy area that's always been problematic. Decorative, functional, or just for fun, amenities and refinements outside your home can increase its living area and value while providing hours of safe, relaxing outdoor living for your family.

Such projects, found throughout this book, can be both easy-to-build and inexpensive. With an understanding of the basics, the right tools for the job, a set of our plans—plus an adequate supply of time and patience—you can turn a corner of your yard or garden into a useful and practical work area or a charming and restful hideaway.

As you flip through the following pages, you'll find more than 100 project plans meant to inspire you to make the most of your outdoor space. Maybe you don't know yet which kind of structure you wish to build or what would add the most character to your yard. That's okay—take your time and browse the plans to figure out which project would best suit your needs.

You'll notice that the different projects have been conveniently organized by type. The sections include: Gazebos & Garden Structures; Sheds; Studios & Cottages; Playhouses & Swingsets; Poolhouses & More; and Decks. Surely at least one of the plans in this collection would help spruce up your property.

This rustic structure can be used as a storage area for lawn and garden equipment or as a handy potting shed. For plan details, see page 62.

Decks offer families an ideal spot to eat, lounge, or socialize. Turn to page 95 to see the large collection of decks available for your home.

ADVANCE PLANNING
Project Selection
The first step is to decide which project to undertake. Keeping in mind the available space in your yard and your budget, look through this book for ideas. The detailed descriptions and renderings of the various outdoor structures on pages 14–119 are sure to spark your imagination. Of all the possibilities, what do your home, your property, and your family need the most? A garden swing? A child's playset? A gazebo? A tool shed? Many designs have various options, so you can customize plans to suit your specific style.

With all the possibilities fresh in your mind, take a slow walk around your property and decide which outdoor structure is the best match in form and function to your family's needs and to your available space and budget. Consider if you have the time and expertise to build the project you've selected or if you will need to involve a licensed contractor for at least part of the work. Once you've made your decisions, turn to page 122 to order the plans you'll need.

Site Selection
Once you order your plans, it's time to start thinking about site selection. Choosing the appropriate place for your structure depends on a number of things: what you're building, its purpose, who's going to use it, its accessibility, and its appeal. For example, if you decide to build

Trellises, such as the one shown here, are among the featured plans in the Gazebos & Garden Structures section, which begins on page 14.

a gazebo, remember that it will likely become the focal point of your property. If you are constructing a playset, select an area that is visible from the house so you can watch the children.

Drainage: If your property has moist areas, it's best to avoid them. You wouldn't want to place a playset or a garden swing, for instance, in an area that remains damp for two or three days after it rains. The alternative is to provide a dry, firm base by adding sand and gravel fill under the project to help drain the site.

Utilities: Plan ahead for any utilities your project may require: electricity or water for sheds, gazebos, and playhouses, or gas for heat or a grill. Always call your local utilities provider for underground cable and water line locations, even if your project does not require utility connections.

BUILDING BASICS

Site Plan

Creating a site plan, or a detailed layout of the project on the property, is important when incorporating a new addition to an existing landscape. A site plan allows you to view in advance the effect a new structure will have when finished. It is important to conceptualize how the new addition blends in with property lines, utilities, other structures, permanent mature plants, land contours, and roads. You also need to consider the visibility of the new structure from vantage points both outside and within your property lines. In addition, local building officials may require a site plan.

Building Permits

When your advance planning and site selection are complete, it's time to obtain the required building permits. Separate building permits are usually needed for each construction discipline: one for the structure, one for the electrical work, one for the plumbing, one for the heating, and so on. Specific requirements for each vary from region to region across the country. Check with your local building officials before you begin your project to determine which permits you need. If your project is small, permits may not be required.

Building Codes

Along with building permits come required building codes, which are usually imposed by county or city governments. Codes ensure your project meets all standards for safety and construction methods. A local inspector will usually check the progress of your project at various stages. There may be more than one inspector, depending on the utilities you incorporate.

Some of the regulated items the inspectors will check include: distance of project from property lines, handrail heights, stair construction, connection methods, footing sizes and depths, materials used, plumbing, electrical and mechanical requirements, and neighborhood zoning regulations.

Tools Checklist

If you are an experienced do-it-yourselfer, you probably have most of the tools needed for the projects in this book. Compare your tool set to the highlighted list on page 8. Most of these tools are available at rental shops, so you can have "the right tool for the job" without permanently adding it to your set.

Gather together the tools you will need for your project before you begin construction. This simple advice is as important as having your building materials and lumber on site in the needed sizes and quantities before you start. The frustration and aggravation you eliminate will be well worth the time it takes to get organized before you begin.

Selecting Lumber

Each project in this book includes a list of the lumber and other building materials necessary for the job. You will need to determine the type of wood you want to use. Many wood species may be used for outdoor structures. Among the most

When working with pressure-treated wood, take these precautions: do not use boards with a visible chemical residue; wear a mask and goggles when sawing treated wood; do not burn treated wood; sweep up and safely dispose of all sawdust and wood scraps.

common are: redwood, western red cedar, Douglas fir, spruce, southern yellow pine, northern pine, and ponderosa pine. Choose a lumber dealer you can rely on to assist you with wood selection—one that will be familiar with the lumber commonly used in your area for outdoor projects. Before you begin, be sure what you want is available locally. If you desire a wood type not normally in stock in your area, you'll pay much more to acquire it.

Lumber is available in various grades determined by the wood's quality, strength, and resistance to decay. For example, redwood is graded as follows (listed from highest to lowest quality): Clear All Heart, Select Heart, Construction Heart, and Merchantable Heart. Any of the last three grades are commonly used in outdoor construction projects.

Lumber in contact with, or even in close proximity to, the ground must be decay-resistant. Select a resistant species, such as redwood or cedar, and treat your lumber with a preservative before using it on your project.

You may wish to select pressure-treated wood, which is available from most lumber dealers and home centers. With pressure-treated wood, preservatives or fire-retardant chemicals have been forced into the lumber fibers to protect it and prolong its durability. Because of these chemicals, pressure-treated wood should not be used if it will come into direct contact with drinking water or with food for humans or animals. Do not use pressure-treated wood for playsets, either.

When working with pressure-treated wood, take these precautions: do not use boards with a visible chemical residue; wear a mask and goggles when sawing treated wood; do not burn treated wood; sweep up and safely dispose of all sawdust and wood scraps. Check with your lumber supplier for additional restrictions and precautions.

Site Preparation

At last, it's time to begin! You've selected the site according to your observations and site plan; you've obtained complete project plans; you've secured all permits; and you've gathered together all code-approved materials and required tools. Now, to help ensure success, follow these important steps so construction will proceed quickly and smoothly.

Drainage: This is an important word to remember when you begin construction. Water must drain away from the foundation or it will pool on structural supports, eventually rotting and weakening them. Furthermore, water-saturated soil beneath footings may not remain firm enough to support the structure.

The easiest way to supply drainage is to slope the ground away from your structure so water will run off naturally. If the ground does not slope naturally, dig a drainage channel or channels to carry water away. Notice where water runoff flows naturally and install trenches there. Another alternative: you may also be able to solve the problem by simply adding gravel and sand.

Remove weeds and turf: Getting weeds out of the way before you begin building makes construction easier. Hoe or pull out weeds in small areas. In larger areas, a small cultivator can be used to turn over the soil. Keep cultivation shallow to avoid bringing weed seeds to the soil surface where they will germinate.

PIERS AND FOUNDATIONS

Piers and foundations are the base of any project. Foundation walls are commonly made by first pouring the footer (or footing) into a ditch that has been excavated to the required depth to meet local codes. The depth, or thickness, of the footer (usually between 8 and 12 inches) will depend on the type of structure being built. Forms are built and the foundation wall is poured on top of the footer.

Alternatively, you may set a block foundation wall on top of the footer.

Piers are formed from concrete, either precast or "pour-your-own." Precast piers are available in various sizes and with drift-pin connections. These can be set on grade or sunken into the ground, depending on the type you select. To pour your own, you may build your own forms from lumber or use ready-made forms of wax-impregnated cardboard that are available in cylinder or block shapes at local home-improvement or lumber supply stores.

ATTACHING A PROJECT TO ITS FOUNDATION

Whether your structure will be sitting on posts or on a foundation wall, any wood within 12 inches of the soil should be treated as required by most codes. By setting metal connectors in poured concrete, you will create a strong connection. The structure will be less susceptible to wood rot than if you simply sink a post in concrete. All connectors should be of the highest quality 16- to 18-gauge hot-dipped galvanized steel. Ensure that all nails, bolts, nuts, and other fittings exposed to the ele-

Your Basic Tool List Should Include:

Brush and Rollers
Carpenter's Level
Carpenter's Square
Chalk Line
Chisel
Circular Saw
Framing Angle
Hammer
Handsaw
Line Level
Nail Set
Paint
Plumb Bob
Power Drill and Screwdriver
Power Jigsaw
Shovel
Socket Set
Tape Measure
Tool Belt
Wheelbarrow

Of the 25 featured decks in this collection, there's bound to be one that'll match your family's needs. Decks can be found on pages 95–119.

ments are also of galvanized steel.

Many additional foundation options are available, such as slab flooring with anchor ties, block walls, and others. The one you need will be indicated in the detailed set of plans for each project.

STANDARD FLOOR CONSTRUCTION

Of the possible structural systems a project may require, platform framing is the easiest and most common method used. In this system, the entire floor frame is constructed first, including the subflooring. The floor surface thus serves as a platform for the structure's walls. If a concrete slab is poured, it acts as the platform instead.

To construct a floor frame, a sill plate, usually a 2x6, is laid flat on top of the foundation wall and attached with anchor bolts. Then the header joists and edge joists are set upright and nailed to the sill plate. Header, edge, and regular joists are all constructed using the same size lumber. The sill plate will usually be a 2x6. Floor joists are normally placed 16 inches on center with splices only occurring above a beam. The subflooring, which goes over the floor joists, extends to the edges of the floor framing structure.

If you are building a gazebo or other structure using 5x4 or 5x2 decking, the joists may attach to the posts or beams with the decking extended to the edge. It may also be modified for railings or columns.

Structural Bracing

For a stronger floor, additional bracing can be provided with blocking or cross-bridging. "Blocking" uses boards the same dimension as the joists, placed between the joists for added support. "Cross-bridging" uses 2x3s or 2x4s placed in an X pattern between joists for added support.

Be sure all joists are installed at the same level, otherwise the surface of the floor will be uneven. To check the joists, place a chalk or string line over them and pull it tight. It will be easy to tell which joists are too high or too low and need to be adjusted.

> Be sure all joists are installed at the same level, otherwise the surface of the floor will be uneven.

Splicing Joists

Joists, like beams, must be spliced if they do not span the entire distance between beams. Splice only above a beam to ensure needed support. Use a wood or metal cleat, or overlap the joist at the beam. Extend the joist 8 inches or more beyond the sides of each beam to increase the junction's strength and to allow room for the splice.

If the floor joist spans more than 8 feet, apply a cross-brace or blocking between joists to prevent twisting. The longer the distance, the more likely the joist is to twist.

Use blocking to support joists that are 2x4, 2x6, or 2x8, but for joists that are 2x10 or larger, install wood or metal cross bracing. If the floor span of your project is 8 feet or less, the end headers normally provide enough support so that cross-bracing is not required.

STANDARD WALL CONSTRUCTION

In platform framing, exterior walls and interior partitions have a single 2x4 plate (2x6 when studs are 2x6s) that rests on the subfloor. This is called the bottom, or sole, plate. The top of the walls have a doubled plate called the top plate, or cap plate, that supports ceiling joists and, in most cases, roof rafters. The structure's walls are usually built lying flat on the subfloor, then raised into position in one section. Wall studs are normally placed 16 inches on center, but if 2x6 studs are used, then 24 inches on center may be acceptable.

Prior to starting the wall construction, be sure to verify all rough opening sizes for doors, windows, etc. All headers above the doors and windows are constructed of 2x material, which is really 1½ inches thick. With two 2x6s or 2x8s (and a ½ inch plywood spacer), you can build a header to support almost any window or door span for the projects in this book.

ROOF FRAMING

Up to the top plate, the construction method depends on the type of framing system used. Above the top plate,

Glossary of Terms

Beam: A horizontal framing member of wood or steel, no less than 5 inches thick and at least 2 inches wider than it is thick.

Board: Any piece of lumber more than 1 inch wide but less than 2 inches thick.

Footer: The portion of a structure's foundation that spreads and transmits the weight directly to the ground.

Foundation: The part of a building that rests on a footing and supports all of the structure above it.

Header: Any structural wood member used across the ends of an opening to support the cut ends of shortened framing members in a floor, wall, or roof.

Joist: A horizontal structural member that, together with other similar members, supports a floor or ceiling system.

Pier: An isolated column used to support weight.

Pitch: A roof's angle or inclination; its rise over run.

Rise: The vertical height from a roof's supports to its ridge.

Run: The distance horizontally between the roof ridge and the outer face of the wall.

R-value: The numerical representation of a material's insulating properties relative to its density or thickness.

Sill Plate: A structural member anchored on top of the foundation wall where the floor joists rest.

Span: The horizontal distance between two supports.

Splice: Connecting two similar materials to another by welding, gluing, lapping, mechanical couplers, or other means.

Stud: The 2x4 or 2x6 vertical member used in wood frame construction.

Top Plate: A member on top of a stud wall where joists rest to form a ceiling or support an additional floor.

Gazebos in various styles, shapes, and sizes are included in this collection. To see which one would be best for your yard, turn to page 14.

Adirondack chairs are timeless backyard favorites and offer novice builders the perfect project to undertake. See page 38 for plan details.

the construction method depends mainly on the style of the roof indicated for the structure.

Two structures built from identical plans can look considerably different when the style of the roof is changed. The two most common roof styles are the gable and the hip. For garden-amenity structures, other styles are also used, such as a shed roof or gambrel roof.

There are five important roof-framing terms that are used in calculating rafter length: span, rise, run, pitch, and pitch line. To construct a roof, you will need to use a rafter square, available from local suppliers. Get either a metal angle or a triangular square. The least expensive model is a plastic triangular square; it comes with instructions on how to use it to measure rafters, cut angles, and cut "the bird's mouth," which is the part that sits on the wall top plate. Because cutting the roof rafters is probably the most

difficult task involved in building a garden structure, the rafter square is the most useful tool you can have.

STAIRS

Most outdoor projects require stairs to provide access from the ground level. Stairs are composed of the tread (the surface you walk on) and the riser (the vertical distance between steps). Stairs are usually 4-, 5-, or 6-feet wide. It is important to retain a constant riser-to-tread ratio. This ensures an equal distance between steps, which prevents missteps and stumbles. A common riser-to-tread ratio is 6:12, which can be built by using two 2x6 treads and a 2x6 riser. For example, if the width of the tread is 12 inches, the next step should "rise" 6 inches.

The supports to which the steps are attached are called stair stringers or the carriage, usually built from a 2x12. Steps can also be constructed as a single step

from floor to ground or from one floor level to another. Some steps are constructed as a separate level, a kind of continuous step, from one floor level to another.

INSULATION

If you are going to heat or cool your structure, you may want to insulate the walls and ceiling. R-values vary according to climate, so check with your local supplier for the requirements in your area. The typical wall insulation is R-19 in cold climates, with R-38 for the ceiling.

NEXT STEP

Now that you've got the basics, you're ready to begin your search. With more than 100 plans showcased in this book, there's likely to be something that's just right for you. But if you'd like to view an even bigger selection of outdoor project plans, log on to www.eplans.com 24 hours a day, seven days a week. ■

Outdoor Project Plans You Can Build

On the following pages are illustrations for 100+ projects—some practical, some whimsical, but all designed to enhance your lifestyle and make creative use of your outdoor areas. Complete construction blueprints are available for you to order for each project. All are ready to build or to have a professional contractor build for you. Each is easily adaptable to almost any style or type of home or outdoor area.

Blueprint packages include everything you or your contractor will need to complete the project—frontal sheet, materials list, floor plan, framing plan, and where needed, elevations. In addition, Home Planners offers a Gazebo Construction Details package, which provides additional information for building gazebos, as well as a Standard Construction Details package, which gives advice on basic building techniques.

Take your time as you look through the following pages. Imagine how each project shown would look in your yard or garden and the enjoyment and convenience it would provide for your family. When you've decided on a project, simply turn to page 122 for order information. We'll rush you the plans so you can get started on your very own outdoor project as soon as possible.

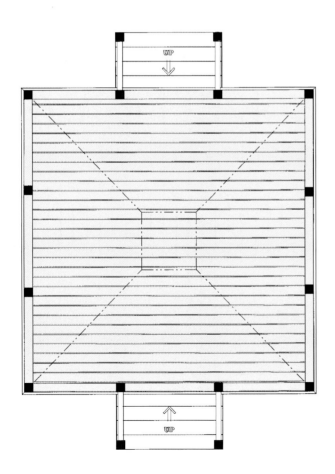

plan# **HPT950001**

Width: 16'-0"
Depth: 22'-4"

SEARCH ONLINE @ EPLANS.COM

Dance the night away in this double-entrance, pass-through-style gazebo. By day, the open-air construction provides a clear view in all directions. The large floor area of 256 square feet seats 12 to 16 people comfortably or nicely accommodates musicians or entertainers for a lawn party. The decorative cupola can be lowered, louvered, or removed to create just the appearance you want. Or, add an antique weathervane just for fun. This gazebo has five steps up, which give it a large crawlspace for access to any added utilities. Its square shape allows for simple cutting and floor framing, plus easy assembly of the roof frame. The trim and handrails are simple to construct or modify to achieve several different design effects.

plan# HPT950002

Width: 12'-0"
Depth: 12'-0"

SEARCH ONLINE @ EPLANS.COM

Best suited for larger lots, this gazebo provides a prime spot for entertaining. With 144 square feet, it has as much surface space as the average family room. And, topping out at just under 17½ feet, it's as tall as a one-story house! Boasting many neoclassic features—perfect proportions, columns, and bases—it blends well with a variety of housing styles: Cape Cod, Georgian, farmhouse, and others. The cupola is an added touch that allows for ventilation. Cedar or redwood would be a good choice for building materials.

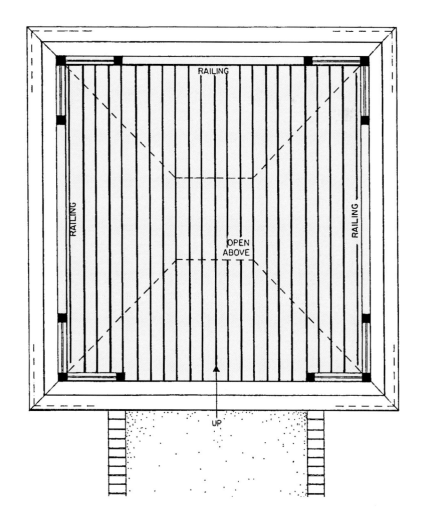

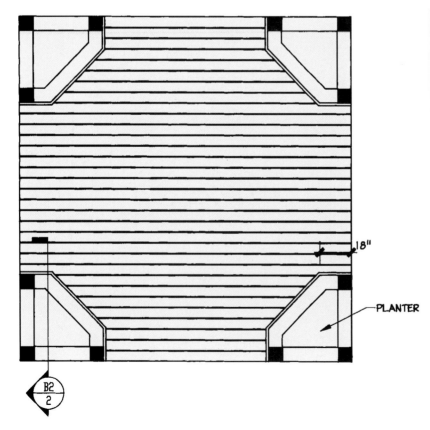

18"

PLANTER

B2
2

plan# HPT950003

Width: 16'-0"
Depth: 16'-0"

SEARCH ONLINE @ EPLANS.COM

The built-in planters and open roof areas of this multiple-entrance gazebo make this design a gardener's dream come true. The open roof allows sun and rain ample access to the planters and gives the structure a definite country-garden effect. Built with or without a cupola, the open lattice work in the walls and roof will complement a wide variety of landscapes and home designs. A creative gardener will soon enhance this charming gazebo with a wealth of plants and vines. Tuck a bird bath or bubbling fountain into a corner to further the garden setting. The large design—256 square feet—ensures that both you and nature have plenty of room to share all this gazebo has to offer. It easily accommodates a table and chairs when you invite your guests to this outdoor hideaway.

plan# HPT950004

Width: 16'-0"
Depth: 14'-10"

SEARCH ONLINE @ EPLANS.COM

Designed in the Craftsman style with exposed rafter tails, this gazebo also features column and pier supports that lend a rustic air to your yard. Add electricity and water to make a perfect garden spot for entertaining. This design features an accented roof overhang and open soffit. The piers can be finished in stucco to complement a Tudor-, Spanish-, or Mission-style home. This two-step-up structure has a vented crawlspace in the base to give quick access to any utilities which might be added. The floor area is approximately 160 square feet and will accommodate eight to 10 people in standard chairs. The double entrance can be modified to a single entrance, with benches added to increase seating to 21.

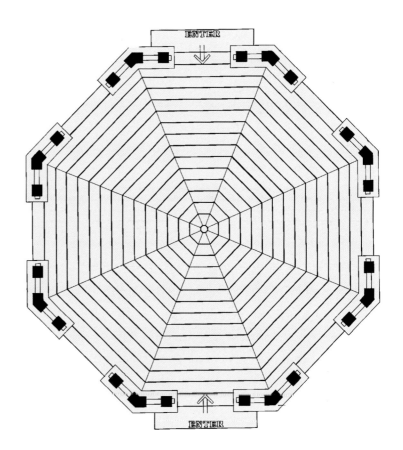

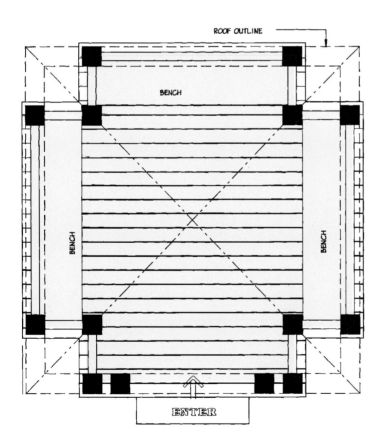

ROOF OUTLINE

BENCH

BENCH

BENCH

ENTER

plan# **HPT950005**

Width: 12'-0"
Depth: 12'-0"

SEARCH ONLINE @ EPLANS.COM

Light and airy, the unique trellis roof of this innovative single-entrance gazebo is just waiting for your favorite perennial vines. Modify the railings to a lattice pattern and train vines or grapes—or roses, for a splash of color—to experience nature all around you. The inset corners of the design provide plenty of space for planting. Simple lines make this delightful gazebo easy to construct, with no cumbersome cutting or gingerbread. The large area—128 square feet—provides built-in seating for nine people. This flexible design could be modified to a closed roof with any standard roof sheathing and shingles, and the single-entrance design can be altered to accommodate multiple entrances.

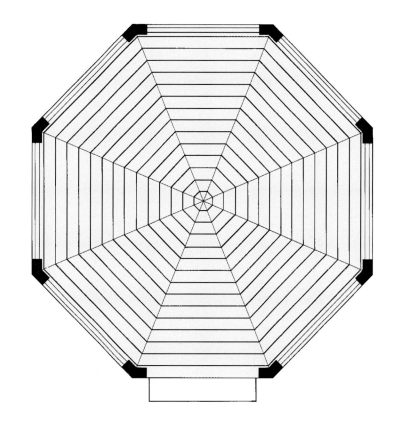

plan# HPT950006

Width: 16'-0"
Depth: 14'-9"

This all-American single-entrance gazebo is simple to construct and easy to adapt to a variety of styles. All materials are available in most areas with no special cutting for trim or rails. This gazebo is distinguished by its simple design and large floor area. The traditional eight-sided configuration and overall area of approximately 181 square feet allow for the placement of furniture with ample seating for eight to 10 people. Build as shown, or modify the trim and railings to give a totally different appearance. If multiple entrance/exit access is desired, simply eliminate the rails as needed. Access to the ground is a single step, which could be easily modified for a low ramp.

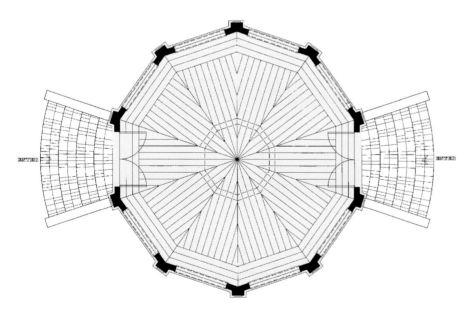

plan# HPT950007

Width: 19'-10"
Depth: 29'-6"

Shining copper on the cupola and shimmering glass windows all around enhance this double-entrance gazebo with dancing light and color. The many windows allow natural light to engulf the interior, making it a perfect studio. Easy to heat and cool, this gazebo contains operable louvers in the cupola to increase the flow of air. An exhaust fan could be added to the cupola to further maximize air flow. The masonry base with brick steps gives the structure a definite feeling of both elegance and permanence. The roof structure is made from standard framing materials with the cupola adorned with a copper cover. If cost is a factor, the cupola roof could be made of asphalt shingles and the glass windows could be eliminated.

plan# HPT950008

Width: 11'-8"
Depth: 11'-8"

This delightful gingerbread-style gazebo will be the focal point of your landscape. The floor area of nearly 144 square feet is large enough for a table and chairs. Or, add built-in benches to increase the seating capacity to accommodate 20 people. Painted white with pink asphalt roof shingles, this gazebo has a cool summery appearance. Or, you can build it with unpainted, treated materials and cedar shake shingles for an entirely different effect. Either exterior design will provide an outstanding setting for years of outdoor relaxation and entertainment. The jaunty cupola complete with spire adds a stately look to this single-entrance structure. The plans also include an optional arbor, which can be incorporated into the entrance of the gazebo.

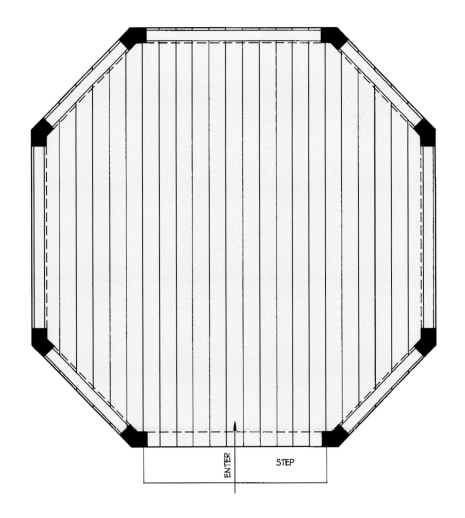

ENTER   STEP

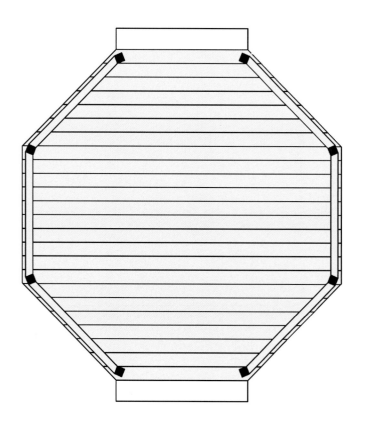

plan# HPT950009

Width: 12'-0"
Depth: 12'-0"

SEARCH ONLINE @ EPLANS.COM

Victorian on a small scale, this gazebo will be the highlight of any yard. With a cupola topped by a weathervane, a railed perimeter, and double steps up, it's the essence of historic design. Small enough to fit on just about any size lot, yet large enough to accommodate a small crowd, it is perfect for outdoor entertaining with 114 square feet of space. Choose standard gingerbread details from your local supplier to make it your own.

ORDER BLUEPRINTS 24 HOURS, 7 DAYS A WEEK, AT 1-800-521-6797

plan# **HPT950010**

Width: 8'-0"
Depth: 8'-0"

SEARCH ONLINE @ EPLANS.COM

A graceful ambiance accents the outer and inner structure of this garden gazebo charmer. Host a summertime picnic and enjoy the alluring shade provided, when mingling with friends and family. An evening get-together can be enhanced by a gazebo dance floor decorated with Chinese lanterns. Set up a table and let the kids enjoy outdoor arts and crafts, safe from the threat of blistering summertime sunburns. With an endless number of possibilities, this outdoor display is a useful and stylish addition to any home landscape.

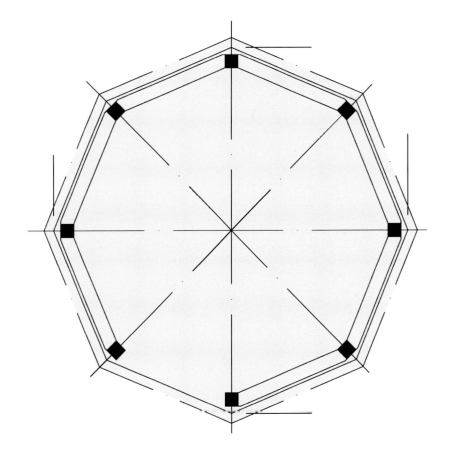

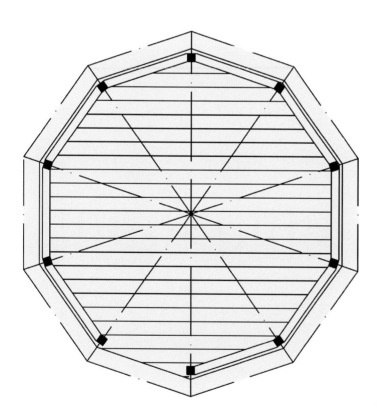

Imagine the big day—a wedding set in the comfort and familiarity of your own backyard. Enchanting and unforgettably romantic, this memorable gazebo is a splendid addition to any garden scene. Family and friends will be dazzled by this 106-square-foot structure—large enough to accommodate a wedding party. Simple, yet elegant, this gazebo will enhance the scenery and add to the allure of any private garden. Benches may be added to offer outdoor covered seating on breezy summer nights.

plan # HPT950012

Width: 5'-10"
Depth: 6'-0"

This charming gazebo, with a simple design and lattice sides and roof accents, will be the highlight of your yard or garden—and its small footprint makes it easy to situate on any lot! Turn it into a comfortable outdoor sitting area by adding patio chairs and a petite table, or add child-sized chairs and let the kids play in the shade. However you use it, this gazebo will add appeal to your property for years to come.

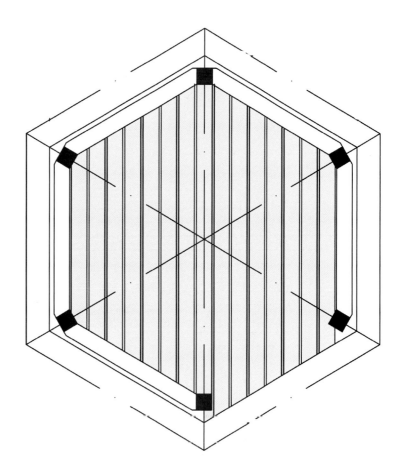

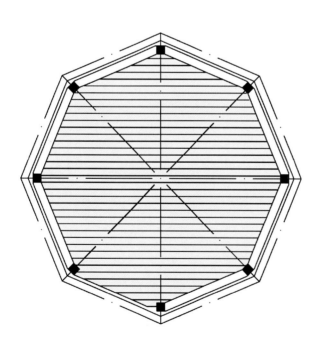

plan# **HPT950013**

Width: 10'-0"
Depth: 10'-0"

SEARCH ONLINE @ EPLANS.COM

Simple, yet brisk—this charming gazebo offers a sheltered openness to any yard display. With 71 square feet, this gazebo is petite, yet elegantly rustic for the countryside setting. This gazebo provides a haven and decorative motif to any garden or outdoor arrangement. Add a table and chairs and enjoy afternoon lemonade or tea over a game of cards. This structure will encourage outdoor leisure activities almost any time of the year.

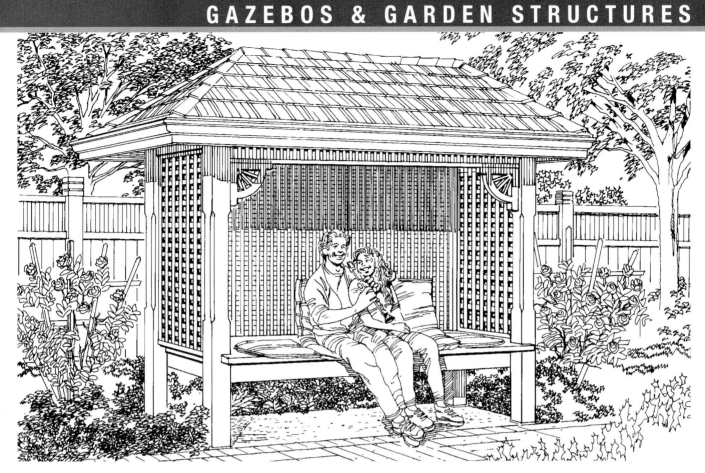

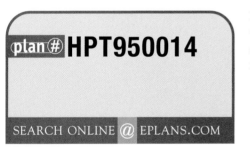

plan# HPT950014

SEARCH ONLINE @ EPLANS.COM

Enjoy the outdoors in your own backyard with a stylish trellis/bench—perfect for any yard or garden setting. This wood-made design features an edged-board bench, lattice screens to train growing vines, and a roof structure for shade. Spend a relaxing afternoon reading or talking with a friend in the peaceful seclusion of your own garden.

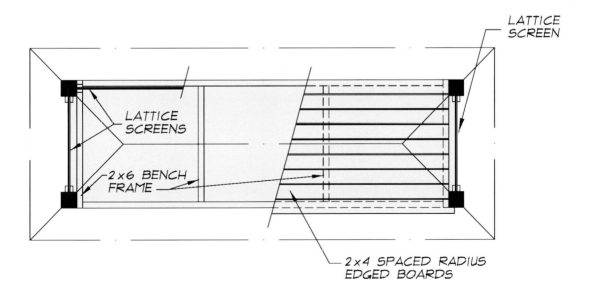

LATTICE SCREEN

LATTICE SCREENS

2 x 6 BENCH FRAME

2 x 4 SPACED RADIUS EDGED BOARDS

Designed for serious entertaining, the size alone—162 square feet—ensures you that this gazebo is unique. The star-lattice railing design, built-in benches, and raised center roof with accent trim make this structure as practical as it is attractive. Large enough for small parties, there is built-in seating for about 20 people and enough floor area for another 10 to 20. Ideal for entertaining, the addition of lights and a wet bar make this design an important extension of any home. The rooflines and overhang can be modified to give a pagoda effect, or removed completely to give a carousel-like appearance. Although this double-entrance, pass-through gazebo looks complicated, it is fairly simple to build with the right tools and materials.

plan# HPT950015

Width: 18'-0"
Depth: 10'-0"

SEARCH ONLINE @ EPLANS.COM

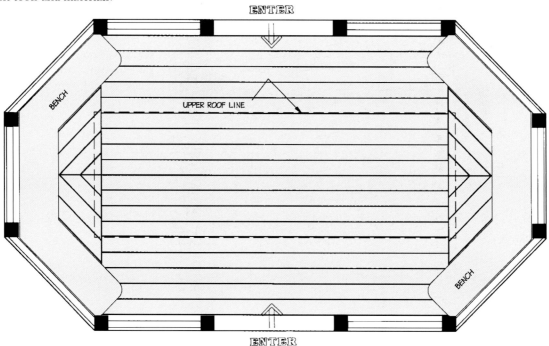

plan# HPT950108

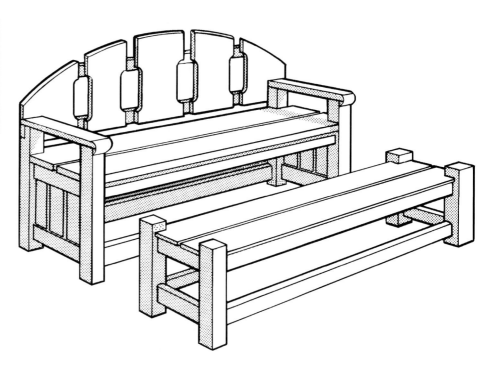

Wide boards and square supports lend a sturdy look to this leisure bench and its accompanying table, while the curved back of the bench adds elegance. Place it on your patio to serve as a more formal alternative to a picnic table—it's wide enough for several people to sit comfortably—or set it in the garden to create a tranquil relaxation spot just for you. Simple step-by-step instructions allow quick and easy construction.

plan# HPT950016

Width: 10'-0"
Depth: 8'-0"

Gazebos, always a striking addition to a garden, bring to mind a wide variety of images—outdoor weddings, elegant parties, and long, relaxing summer afternoons. Get started on creating your own pleasant images and memories with this lovely four-sided gazebo! The gabled roof offers plenty of shade, allowing you a comfortable place for outdoor entertaining. Dress it up with hanging or potted plants, or leave it unadorned for a classic look.

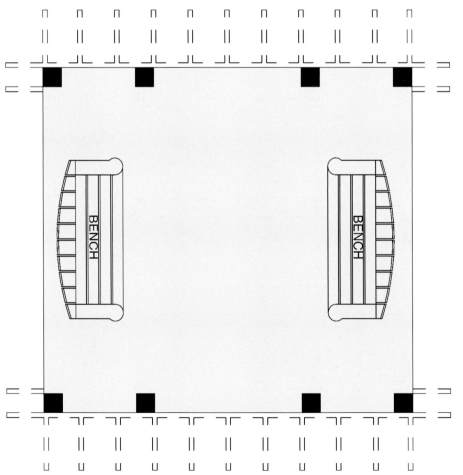

BENCH

BENCH

plan# HPT950017

Width: 12'-0"
Depth: 12'-9"

Timeless elegance is the theme to this garden beauty. One romantic evening or a comfortable, leisurely afternoon spent underneath this trellis will entice anyone to relax, and it encourages more fresh-air outings into your own backyard. Constructed with wood-screened lattices on every side, this enclosed, shaded haven provides a peaceful escape into the outdoors. Vines can be trained to grow along the sides or above to offer extra shade and an enchanting atmosphere.

plan# HPT950018

Width: 7'-0"
Depth: 7'-0"

Acting as an elegant garden tunnel, this stylish trellis is a beautiful addition to any private yard display. Placed at the beginning or end of any brick or cobblestone pathway, this structure gracefully enhances any entrance or exit. Green garden vines may be trained to sprawl up, down, or across the interwoven side lattices. The wooden material will accent any rustic-made environment. The trellis is topped off and connected by a flat lattice, which naturally shades any time of the year.

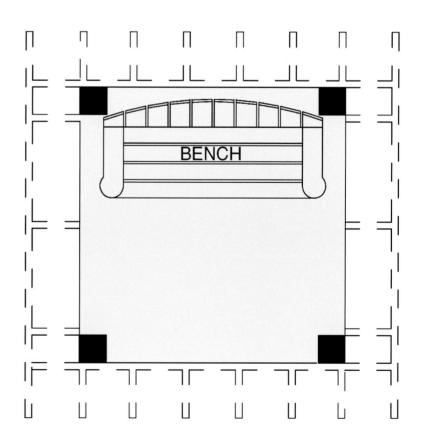

BENCH

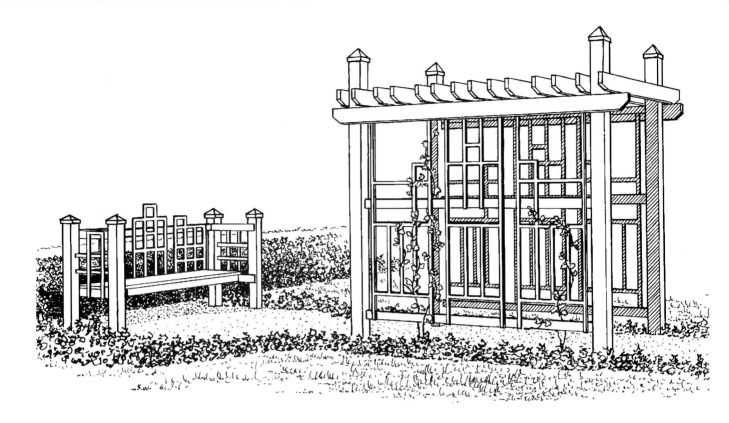

Build this impressive arbor to cover a garden path or walkway. Add the matching bench inside the arbor as a plant shelf or to provide shaded seating. Use the bench outside as an accent to both the arbor and the surrounding landscape. The 7'-11" patterned back and 5'-11" x 8'-11/2" trellis roof are ideal for climbing vines or roses, giving this beautiful arbor even more of a garden effect. The 8'-11" bench is wide enough to seat four or five adults comfortably. The latticework design is repeated on the back and sides of the bench. The arbor is designed to sit on a slab, or you can sink the support columns right into the ground using pressure-treated materials.

plan# **HPT950019**

SEARCH ONLINE @ EPLANS.COM

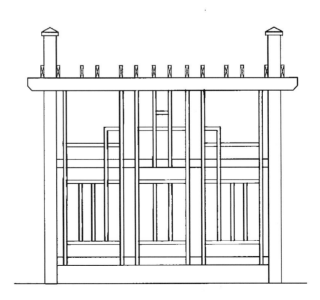

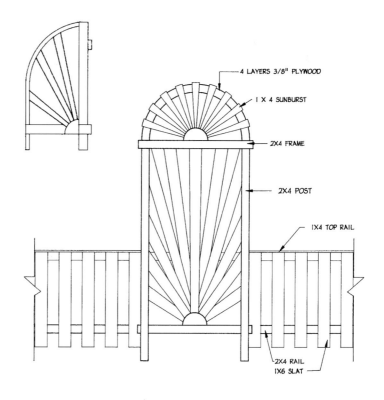

plan# HPT950020

A distinctive sunburst pattern is repeated in each element of this attractive and versatile eight-foot garden arbor. Train your favorite vines over the slat roof to provide shade for the flower beds below or for the roses climbing along the slat-fence extensions. Also included in this package are plans for a four-foot corner trellis, which can be used to extend the sunburst pattern to other areas of your landscape and serve as an accent in flower beds or planters. This arbor—with its sunburst effect—offers a warm and welcoming focal point to any yard or garden area.

4 LAYERS 3/8" PLYWOOD

I X 4 SUNBURST

2X4 FRAME

2X4 POST

IX4 TOP RAIL

2X4 RAIL

1X6 SLAT

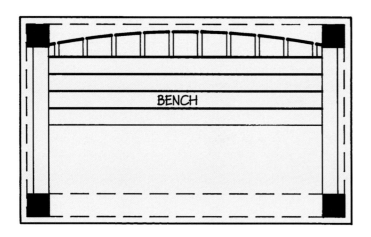

BENCH

plan # HPT950021

Width: 6'-0"
Depth: 3'-6"

SEARCH ONLINE @ EPLANS.COM

You can create a cozy shaded nook for reading or relaxing with this appealing strombrella. It's simple to build as a glider or with a fixed seat. Either option provides ample room for two or three people to sit comfortably. Both designs use standard materials. For a fixed unit, attach it to a cement slab. To make it moveable, use a wood base. Cover the roof with basic asphalt or fiberglass shingles, or use cedar shake shingles to enhance the appearance.

plan# HPT950022

Width: 12'-0"
Depth: 8'-0"

An accent to gracious living, this classic strombrella will create an elegant focal point in any garden or landscape. Evoking memories of a more slowly paced era, the design is similar to those built in the late 1800s. The bench is large enough to seat up to six people. To increase its function, a half-round pole table could be added to provide a small picnic area or a nook for reading, cards, or quiet conversation. The millwork can be purchased from your local supplier or from the manufacturer listed on the construction drawings. The generous entrance is four feet wide and could provide space for additional seating if needed. You can build this structure with a wood base to allow for movable feasts, or secure it to a slab to make it permanent.

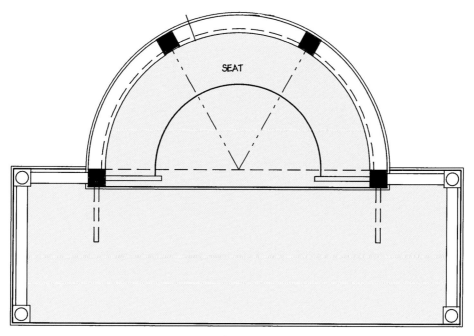

SEAT

Combine form, function, and beauty in this appealing bridge to enhance your landscape and provide easy passage over wet or rocky terrain. Entrance and exit ramps at either end of the bridge replicate the gentle arch of the handrail. The plans for this functional addition show how to build six-, eight- or 10-foot spans to meet your needs. The decorative railing pattern will add a touch of Folk Victorian elegance and charm to any site.

plan# **HPT950023**

SEARCH ONLINE @ EPLANS.COM

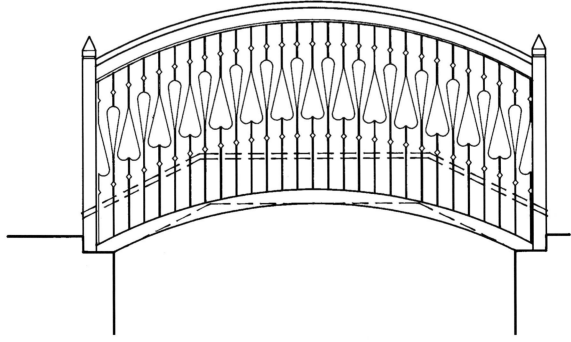

plan# **HPT950024**

Nostalgia unlimited—this romantic covered bridge will re-create a unique link to history on your site. It is patterned after functional bridges built in the 1700s and 1800s, which were intended to provide a dry resting place for weary travelers. This current-day design offers expandable dimensions for a 12-foot, 14-foot or 16-foot span. To cross a wider area, the span can be increased by multiples of those dimensions, using larger floor joists. Check with your local supplier for the span capability of the joists you employ in your project. The sides of this "glimpse into the past" have open window areas to allow air to flow freely. The generous width allows for safe passage of any standard garden tractor or mower.

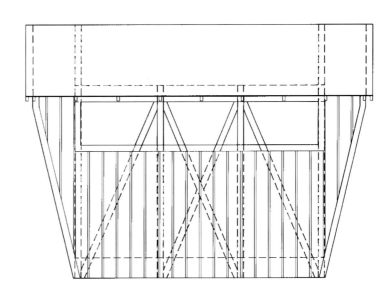

Picture yourself relaxing in this charming Adirondack chair—you can almost feel the warm summer breeze and taste the lemonade. The signature curved footrest aligns perfectly with the seat of the chair to provide perfect comfort for your legs and back. Wide side rests accommodate your arms and a cold drink. The deep seat bed will allow space for a cushion, should you choose to fashion one to fit. Build one just for yourself or enough for your entire family—they're sure to want their own once they've spied yours. Back is 40" high.

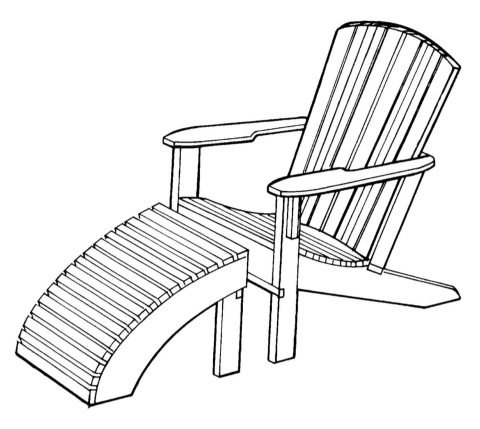

Your backyard will become the favorite hangout of friends and neighbors once you install this charming garden swing—everyone loves to enjoy the outdoors in style! The six-foot bench offers enough space to seat several people, and a wide canopy provides shade from the sun on hot summer days. Five feet wide and over seven feet high, the canopy also allows a bit of extra space for other guests to step into the shade.

plan # HPT950109

This project offers two different picnic table designs. The rectangular design measures 72" x 60" x 30" and seats six adults or eight children comfortably. The octagonal design at 56" x 56" offers seating for eight in a smaller area. The four angled benches allow gentle access by avoiding having to step over the bench to sit down at the table. Both designs sit well on any patio, deck, or lawn.

plan # HPT950027

Width: 8'-0"
Depth: 8'-0"

Looking for a memorable addition to your yard or garden? Station this charming outdoor structure at the entry, and gain admiring attention from passers-by! For an elegant old-fashioned look, plant graceful vines and allow them to twine around the structure's posts, railings, and roof. A bench on each side offers a place to sit and bask in the sun.

plan# HPT950110

Do you have too much clutter in your garage? Then you definitely need one of these! This gabled storage shed features plenty of space to store all your extras. The radius window above the door adds extra light to the inside along with style. This project is designed with a wood floor on concrete footing.

plan# HPT950028

Width: 12'-0"
Depth: 12'-0"

Rustic barn-like detail makes this garden structure so much more than a storage shed. A split barn door, a "hay-loft" balcony, and a gambrel roofline add charm and style—and make it the perfect addition to your rural estate. A wood ramp leads up to the single entry door; an incline ladder stretches to the balcony loft. Paint it red for a true barn or stable facade. For storage or hobbies, this is one outdoor building you'll come to love.

plan# HPT950029

Width: 12'-0"
Depth: 8'-0"

Barnyard charm is captured in this smaller lawn-shed version. Vertical wood siding and barnyard-style double doors can accommodate large machinery comfortably. This lawn shed can also act as a home storage extension. Workshop tools and other garden supplies can also be accommodated inside this 96-square-foot structure. A single window at the rear illuminates the inside. Flower beds may be added outside to decorate and blend this structure more comfortably into the home garden scene.

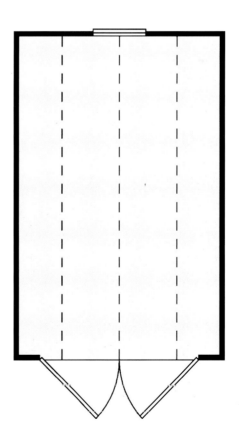

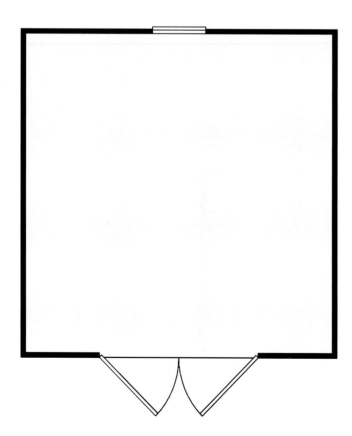

Country living is complete with this barn-yard-style shed, which complements any country or farmhouse setting as a quaint rural motif. Double doors open to accommodate and house any large lawn machinery. Inside this 144-square-foot wood-siding structure, space can be divided for tool storage, wood stock storage, or even a small outdoor workshop area. A window at the rear of the barn shed illuminates the inside for extra light, making it easier to maneuver inside during the day.

plan# HPT950031

Width: 8'-0"
Depth: 8'-0"

SEARCH ONLINE @ EPLANS.COM

Rustic and efficient style is plentiful and apparent in this quaint countryside design. Reflecting well upon a farmhouse scene, this barnyard shed boasts simplicity, and a useful country charm. Through double doors, an expandable interior can easily house the lawn mower, yard equipment, or potting supplies for the family garden. The 96-square-foot interior can be used differently throughout the year as seasons change. Keep a wood stock pile dry in the winter for firewood. In the spring, utilize the interior space for planting supplies. Keep extra lawn chairs available in the summer. And keep bagged raked leaves from blowing over in the fall.

This spacious, yet traditional lawn design is ideal for storage of large yard equipment. Traditional wood siding and a rear sloped ceiling define this rustic exterior. Inside, 144 square feet can be divided among yard machinery such as lawn mowers, garden tools, or even additional storage space for homes without an attic or ample indoor storage. This structure is even large enough to accommodate a workshop—perfect for the family handyman.

ptan# **HPT950032**

Width: 19'-11"
Depth: 12'-0"

SEARCH ONLINE @ EPLANS.COM

ORDER BLUEPRINTS 24 HOURS, 7 DAYS A WEEK, AT 1-800-521-6797

plan# HPT950033

Width: 12'-0"
Depth: 12'-0"

Storage space abounds is this simple, yet efficiently structured lawn shed. With the look of a petite home, this wood-siding structure is a charming addition to any family yard. Tools, garden supplies, outdoor equipment, and even firewood can be accommodated with extra room to spare. The interior is well·lit by a single window, and built-ins such as benches, tool cabinets, or shelves can be added to further utilize the space.

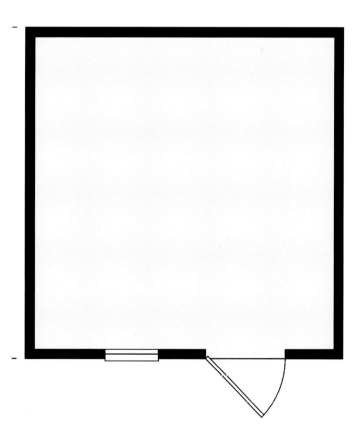

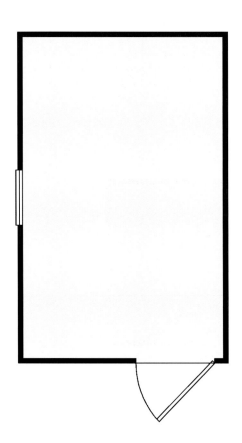

Petite, practical, and perfectly blended with any neighborhood yard, this lawn shed is designed for style and efficiency. The outer facade is graced with traditional wood siding and is accented by a barnyard-style door. Inside, 96 square feet expand the interior for all sorts of garden tools and yard supplies. The sloped ceiling adds a soft finesse to the structural appearance, and a single window brightens the interior. This outdoor storage space is a charming addition to any rustic environment.

plan# **HPT950035**

Width: 8'-0"
Depth: 6'-0"

This modern-day shed design is an efficient structure for any backyard. A wooden plank exterior encloses 48 square feet of storage space, which can be utilized in a number of various ways. Garden tools will abound in the spacious interior and firewood will be kept dry through the winter. Double doors open wide enough to house larger machinery, such as a lawn mower. The sloped ceiling enhances the modern exterior. A flower bed may be a quaint decorative choice to add colorful spice to the outside, while built-in shelves may be added inside to help maintain efficiency of space.

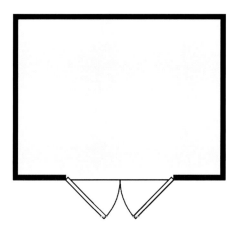

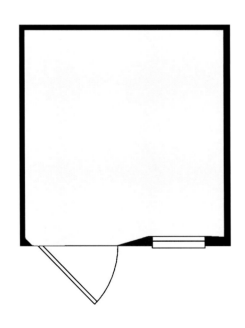

plan# HPT950036

Width: 8'-0"
Depth: 8'-0"

Designed for optimum efficiency with minimal space, this petite lawn enhancer is the charming answer to all your yard and garden needs. Wood siding blends well with farmhouse and traditional home designs and is well suited to any green environment. Inside, 64 square feet provide ample storage space. Outside, decorative potted plants can be added to enhance the exterior. A quaint door and window compliment this design, which can easily be made into an outdoor playhouse.

plan# **HPT950037**

Width: 12'-0"
Depth: 8'-0"

Rectangular shaping enhances the length and size of this 96-square-foot lawn shed. Wood siding frames the outer structure, which reflects most traditional home exteriors. A single window brightens the interior; notice there is plenty of space for large outdoor equipment. Not only will this structure house yard tools and garden supplies, but other recreational equipment such as bicycles, snow sleds, and skis can also be accommodated.

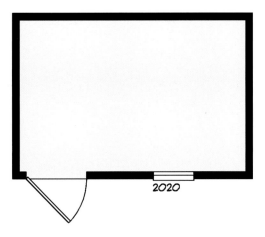

2020

Horizontal wood siding encloses 240 square feet of storage space inside this traditional lawn shed design. A single door and window illuminate the plan throughout. Space may be divided up among gardening tools, yard supplies, firewood, and perhaps even a workshop area. One section of the lawn shed may be opened to offer space and convenience to larger yard machinery such as lawn mowers. This design is sure to blend into any countryside scene and is a great addition to the family property.

plan# **HPT950038**

Width: 20'-0"
Depth: 12'-0"

SEARCH ONLINE @ EPLANS.COM

This design is meant for the efficient yard organizer. Structured with vertical wood siding and a barnyard-style door, this design thrives in any type of country setting and complements many farmhouse designs as well. Inside, a single window brightens the interior, while 240 square feet of space may be divided among a variety of different yard supplies. Gardening tools and chemicals may be stored safely and efficiently away from the home. Extra firewood may be staked inside or outside during long winter periods. Special yard machinery and tools may be accessed and stored in a separate shed area for convenient use.

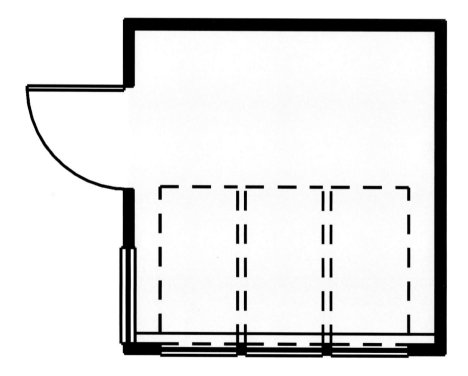

plan# **HPT950040**

Width: 10'-0"
Depth: 10'-0"

Horizontal siding and a steeply sloped roof highlight this eye-catching shed, and the rustic look of the siding is echoed by the wood floor inside. Its compact footprint makes it perfect for storing lawn equipment and gardening tools—or, if you choose, take advantage of the plentiful windows and use it as a greenhouse, so you can enjoy year-round gardening.

plan# HPT950041

Width: 16'-0"
Depth: 12'-0"

Vertical siding, a gently sloping roof, and a charming boxed window make this convenient shed the perfect companion for your country home. The interior is naturally lit by the boxed window and a side window, making the shed a good place to store potted plants when the weather grows cooler. With a height of eight feet, the handy overhead door allows easy storage of bicycles, lawn equipment, or even a small boat.

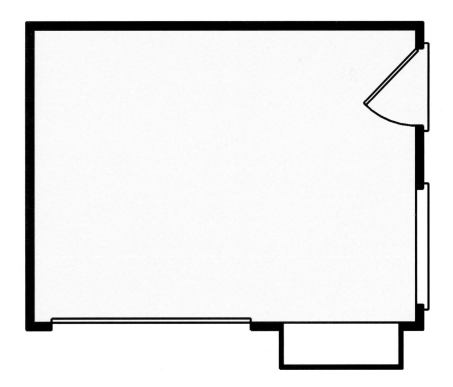

plan# HPT950042

Width: 12'-0"
Depth: 10'-0"

SEARCH ONLINE @ EPLANS.COM

This garden shed, entered through a two-part Dutch door, makes an ideal greenhouse or hobby house with its skylight windows for optimal plant growth. Inside you will find ample room for tool and lawn equipment storage. Whether you are a new or avid gardener, the unique design of this garden shed offers the ultimate in yard flexibility.

plan# HPT950111

Width:12'-0"
Depth: 8'-0"

SEARCH ONLINE @ EPLANS.COM

Here's another appealing playhouse—this one, with a high roof peak and a bit more room, can double as a storage shed, too! The side-gabled roof and just a few touches of country style—a shuttered window, a flower box, and a Dutch door—allow this structure to blend easily with many home styles. Simple to build, this plan is a great addition to any backyard.

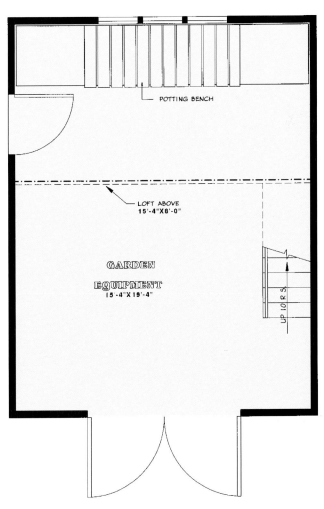

POTTING BENCH

LOFT ABOVE
15'-4"X8'-0"

GARDEN
EQUIPMENT
15'-4"X19'-4"

UP 10 R S

plan# HPT950043

Width: 16'-0"
Depth: 20'-0"

This large multi-level garden shed can be easily modified to become a boat house if yours is a nautical family. As a lawn or garden shed, there is ample room for all your garden equipment, with a separate area for potting plants. The roomy loft provides 133 square feet of safe storage area for chemicals, fertilizers, or other lawn-care products. This practical structure can also be used as a studio or, placed at the water's edge, it can be easily converted to a boat house by adding 4' x 4' columns used as piers in lieu of the slab floor.

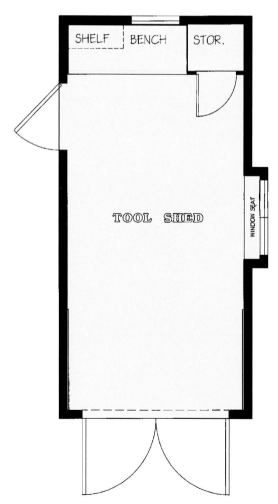

SHELF | BENCH | STOR.

TOOL SHED

WINDOW SEAT

plan# **HPT950044**

Width: 8'-0"
Depth: 16'-0"

SEARCH ONLINE @ EPLANS.COM

Lawn shed extraordinaire, this appealing 128-square-foot design can be easily converted from the Tudor style shown here to match just about any exterior design you prefer. In addition to serving as a lawn shed, this versatile structure also can be used as a craft studio, a pool house, or a delightful playhouse for your children. The double doors and large floor area provide ample access and storage capacity for lawn tractors and other large pieces of equipment. A handy built-in work bench offers needed space for potting plants or working on craft projects. A separate storage room for craft supplies, lawn-care products, or pool chemicals can be locked for safety. Strategically placed on your site, this charming building could be designed to be a reflection of your home in miniature.

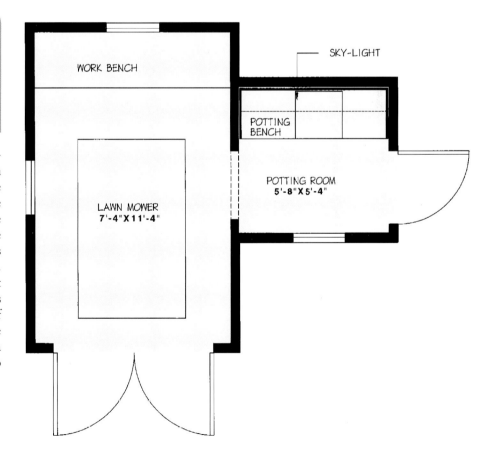

plan# HPT950045

Width: 14'-0"
Depth: 12'-0"

SEARCH ONLINE @ EPLANS.COM

Open the double doors of this multipurpose, 168-square-foot structure and it's a mini-garage for garden tools. Enter by the single door, and it's a potting shed. The tool-shed section is large enough to house the largest lawn tractor, with room to spare for other garden equipment such as shovels, rakes, lawn trimmers, and hoses. With windows on all sides and a skylight above the potting bench, the interior has plenty of natural light; the addition of electrical wiring would make this structure even more practical. The design is shown in a Victorian style, but can be modified to match any gable-roof home design.

WORK BENCH

SKY-LIGHT

POTTING
BENCH

POTTING ROOM
5'-8" X 5'-4"

LAWN MOWER
7'-4" X 11'-4"

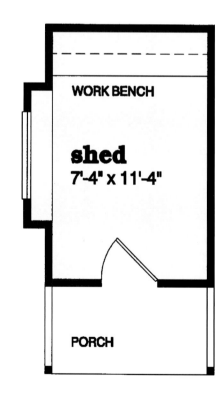

WORK BENCH

shed
7'-4" x 11'-4"

PORCH

plan # HPT950046

Width: 8'-0"
Depth: 16'-0"

SEARCH ONLINE @ EPLANS.COM

A rustic blend of cedar shingles and siding accents the exterior of this stylish yard shed. A couple quick steps lead up to the covered front porch, where a charming window door takes you inside. The interior is enhanced by a large bumped-out window, which illuminates every corner. A built-in work bench is an efficient addition to this design. The whole plan can be utilized for a private workshop—or make it an extra storage space for seasonal outdoor equipment.

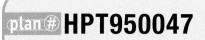

plan # HPT950047

Width: 10'-0"
Depth: 12'-0"

No words quite convey everything this generous storage shed/covered patio combination has to offer. Grooved plywood siding and a shingled double roof are accented by double doors, shutters at the window, a birdhouse tucked in the eaves, and a trellis for your favorite climbers. And if that's not enough, the extended roofline covers a 10' x 10' patio area complete with graceful support columns and topped by a jaunty cupola.

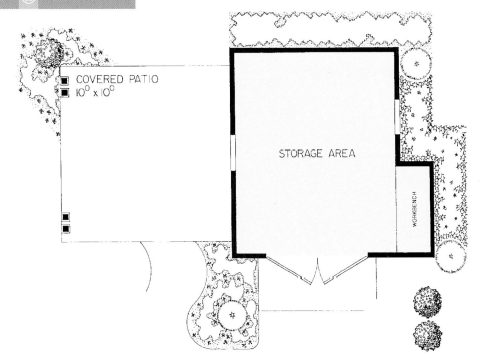

COVERED PATIO
10⁰ x 10⁰

STORAGE AREA

WORKBENCH

The kids will love this one! This functional, practical lawn shed doubles in design and capacity as a delightful playhouse complete with a covered porch, lathe-turned columns, and a window box for young gardeners. The higher roofline on the shed gives the structure a two-story effect, while the playhouse design gives the simple lawn shed a much more appealing appearance. The shed is accessed through double doors. The playhouse features a single-door entrance from the porch and three bright windows. The interior wall between the shed and playhouse could be moved another two-and-a-half feet back to make one of the rooms larger. Remove the interior wall completely to use the entire area exclusively for either the lawn shed or playhouse. The open eaves and porch columns give the structure a country appearance; however, by boxing in the eaves and modifying the columns, you can create just about any style you or the kids like best.

plan# **HPT950048**

Width: 16'-0"
Depth: 8'-0"

SEARCH ONLINE @ EPLANS.COM

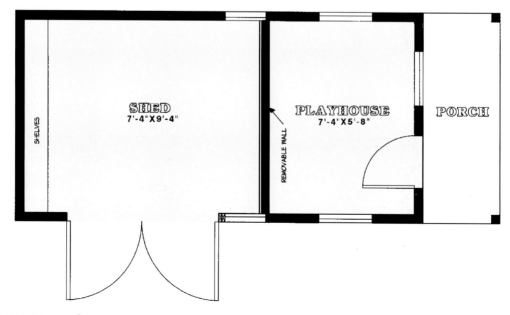

ORDER BLUEPRINTS 24 HOURS, 7 DAYS A WEEK, AT 1-800-521-6797

plan# HPT950049

Width: 16'-0"
Depth: 12'-0"

SEARCH ONLINE @ EPLANS.COM

Efficient for Mom and Dad, while munchkin-sized for the kids, this structure boasts practicality and playfulness. The exterior dazzles in wood siding and cedar shingles—a pleasant display for any outdoor scenery. The garden storage area is separated from the playhouse by a wall and features a sufficient work bench and an illuminating side window. The playhouse resembles a petite version of a country cottage. A tiny covered porch with a wood railing and a window accent the outside and welcome young ones into the petite hideaway. Inside, another window graces the right wall and brightens the interior. There is room enough for a small table and chairs and, most importantly, plenty of toys.

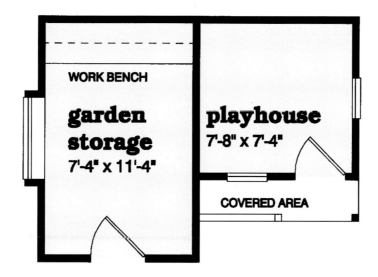

WORK BENCH

garden storage
7'-4" x 11'-4"

playhouse
7'-8" x 7'-4"

COVERED AREA

Designed to blend into the garden surroundings, this cozy little building keeps all your garden tools and supplies at your fingertips. You can vary the materials to create the appearance best suited to your site. This 72-square-foot structure is large enough to accommodate a potting bench, shelves, and an area for garden tools.

plan# **HPT950050**

Width: 12'-0"
Depth: 6'-0"

SEARCH ONLINE @ EPLANS.COM

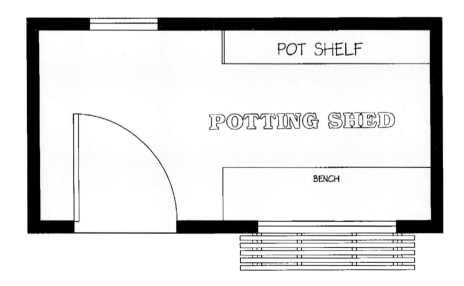

POT SHELF

POTTING SHED

BENCH

ALTERNATE EXTERIOR

plan# HPT950051

Width: 12'-0"
Depth: 16'-0"

SEARCH ONLINE @ EPLANS.COM

For a bare-essentials outdoor structure, this 144-square-foot, weekend cottage offers a wealth of options for its use. Choose it for handy home office space, craft cottage space, extra room for visitors, a playhouse for the kids, or a game room. It features a covered front porch and offers two lovely rustic exteriors for you to choose from. The interior has built-in bunk beds, a closet, and a bumped-out window that works well for table space. Plans include details for both crawlspace and slab foundations.

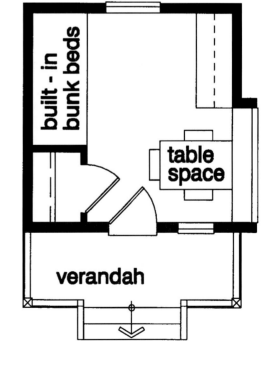

QUOTE ONE®

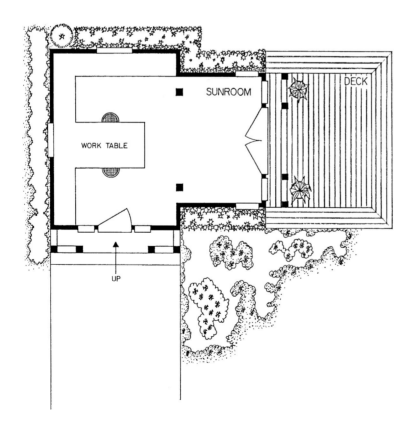

plan# **HPT950052**

Width: 20'-0"
Depth: 16'-0"

SEARCH ONLINE @ EPLANS.COM

The ultimate luxury for any craft enthu-siast—a separate, free-standing building dedicated to your craft of choice! Functional as well as a beautiful addition to your landscape, this cottage provides ample counter space and shelving to spread out or store all your materials and tools. And at break time, relax from your hobby in the attached sunroom with a vaulted ceiling, French doors, and lots of elegant windows. A built-in and well-thought-out work table is flanked by addi-tional countertop work space.

HPT950053

Width: 20'-0"
Depth: 22'-0"

SEARCH ONLINE @ EPLANS.COM

This versatile design features a unique siding pattern: a little bit of country with a pinch of contemporary sophistication. You can build this 320-square-foot, multipurpose structure on a slab or crawlspace or even with a basement! Planned to take advantage of natural light from all sides, this design will make a perfect studio, game room, or office. Or, add a shower in the half-bath and it becomes a guest house. Features include a kitchen large enough for a stove and refrigerator and a utility room with ample space for a furnace and hot-water tank. With all the amenities provided, you could work or relax here for days without ever leaving! The front porch area is a charming place to relax and put your feet up as you or your guests contemplate the events of the day.

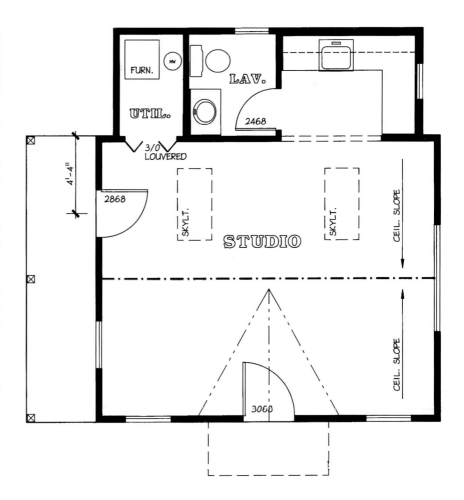

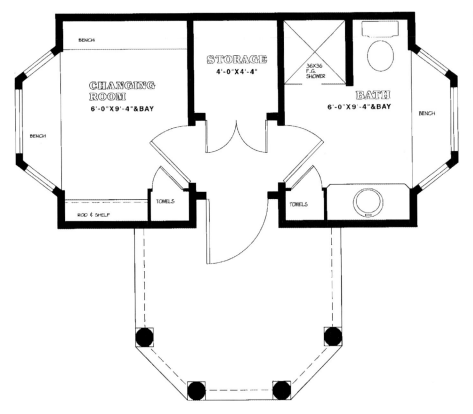

SEARCH ONLINE @ EPLANS.COM

plan# HPT950054

Width: 21'-4"
Depth: 18'-0"

This 383-square-foot pool pavilion offers a changing room and an elegant porch for shade. Add the convenience of bathroom facilities and you're set for outdoor living all summer long. It's designed to provide maximum function in a small area and features built-in benches, shelves, hanging rods, and a separate linen closet for towels. The opaque diamond-patterned windows decorate the exterior of the changing area and the mirror-image bath. The bath could also be made into a kitchen area, then simply add a sliding window to allow easy passage of refreshments to your family and guests at poolside. When you've had enough sun or socializing, recline in the shade under the columned porch, and enjoy a good book or a nap.

HPT950055

Width: 22'-0"
Depth: 24'-0"

SEARCH ONLINE @ EPLANS.COM

A wide porch graces the entry to this 528-square-foot cottage plan, providing a compact, but fully functional apartment. Mill-turned columns support the roof overhang and the front door opens into the generous living room. A kitchen nook has room for a table and chairs and plenty of overhead cabinets. More storage is available in the bedroom—a large closet with folding doors. A full bath with a tempered glass shower and a linen closet in the hall make this a perfect apartment for an elderly parent or a not-quite-ready-to-leave-home teen.

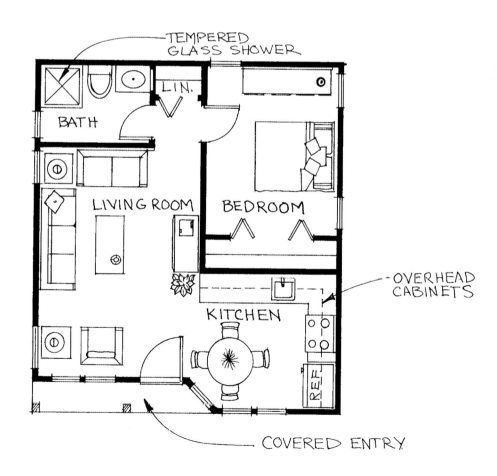

TEMPERED GLASS SHOWER

LIN.

BATH

LIVING ROOM

BEDROOM

OVERHEAD CABINETS

KITCHEN

REF.

COVERED ENTRY

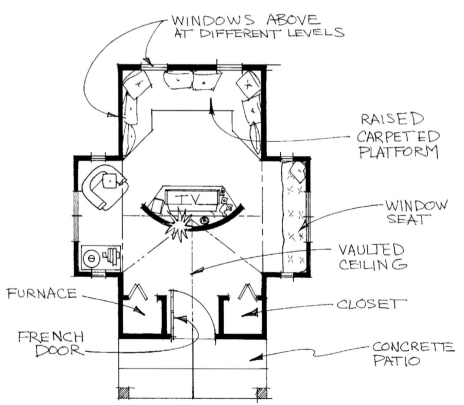

WINDOWS ABOVE
AT DIFFERENT LEVELS

RAISED
CARPETED
PLATFORM

WINDOW
SEAT

VAULTED
CEILING

CLOSET

CONCRETE
PATIO

TV

FURNACE

FRENCH
DOOR

plan# **HPT950056**

Width: 16'-0"
Depth: 22'-0"

SEARCH ONLINE @ EPLANS.COM

Lucky are the teenagers who have the option of staking claim to this private retreat! The overall dimensions of 16' x 22' provide 352 square feet of space for study, TV, or just hanging out. Special features include a raised, carpeted platform in the TV lounge; a comfy window seat for reading or a catnap; a separate niche for electronic games; and a unique, brightly painted graffiti wall in the entryway. Wired for sound, bright colors and windows in a variety of shapes mark this specially designed, free-standing building as teens-only territory.

E. REINKE

Start small with this elegant, 324-square-foot, free-standing garden room. Use the space as a garden retreat for reading or music, or as an arts-and-crafts studio. Two tall, arched windows topped with fanlights grace three sides. A window and entry door flanked by narrow mock shutters are found in the front. The vented cupola and weathervane centered on the cedar-shake roof add an air of rustic charm. To expand the living area an additional 664 square feet, extend the floor plan to each side. Add an entry foyer and full bath to one side of the existing structure and a breakfast nook with its own door to the garden on the other. Existing windows become doorways and, in one case, a window is replaced by an interior wall.

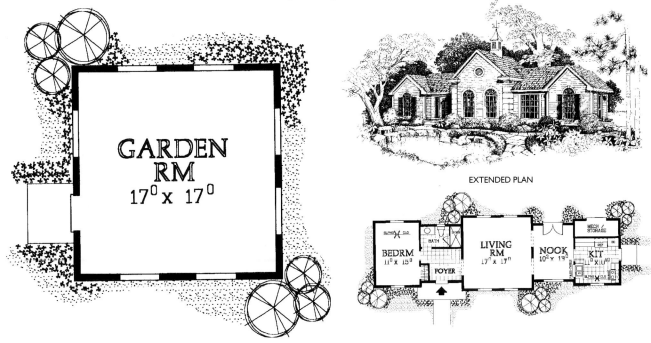

GARDEN RM
17⁰ x 17⁰

EXTENDED PLAN

BEDRM
11⁰ x 15⁰

BATH

LIVING RM
17⁰ x 17⁰

NOOK
10² x 13⁰

KIT
11⁰ x 11⁴⁰

MECH / STORAGE

FOYER

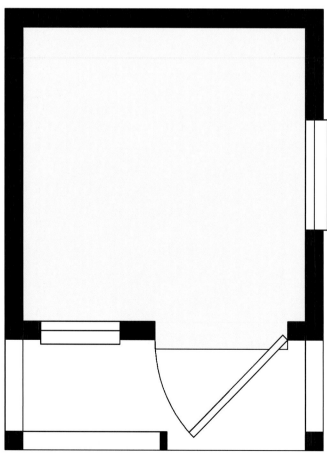

plan# **HPT950058**

Width: 6'-0"
Depth: 8'-0"

This playhouse paradise is an outdoor haven for any youngster looking for self-made entertainment. It's a place your kids can call their own. Similar to a storybook cottage, make-believe games will become a reality. From the quaint covered porch with a wood railing and square supports, go inside to where this clubhouse is brightly illuminated by two windows. This roomy space can be filled with toy furniture, games, arts and crafts, or anything to entertain on a rainy day.

plan # HPT950059

Width: 8'-0"
Depth: 13'-0"

This large, 80-square-foot Victorian playhouse is for the kid in all of us. With space enough to hold bunk beds, use it for overnight adventures. Young children will spend hours playing in this little house. Older kids will find it a haven for quiet study or a perfect private retreat. Four windows flood the interior with natural light, and a single-door entrance provides access from the porch. The overall height will accommodate most adults and the addition of electricity and water would expand the versatility of this unit. Designed on a concrete slab, this playhouse could be placed on a wooden frame for future relocation or change in function after the kids leave home.

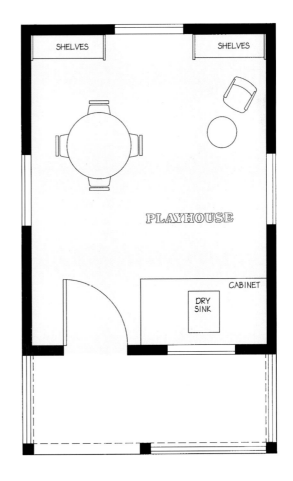

This whimsical, 111-square-foot, scaled-down version of a full-size house makes a dream-come-true playhouse for kids. Featuring a wraparound front porch with a trellis roof, a "real" front door, and a loft that can only be reached by a ladder through a trap door! Generous dimensions provide plenty of space for a playroom and a bunk room. A loft overlooks the main play area. Natural light floods all areas of this delightful play center through windows in the playroom, bunk room, and loft. A sturdy railing borders the loft, and the built-in bunk beds in the bunk room are ready and waiting for sleepovers.

plan# **HPT950060**

Width: 18'-0"
Depth: 14'-0"

SEARCH ONLINE @ EPLANS.COM

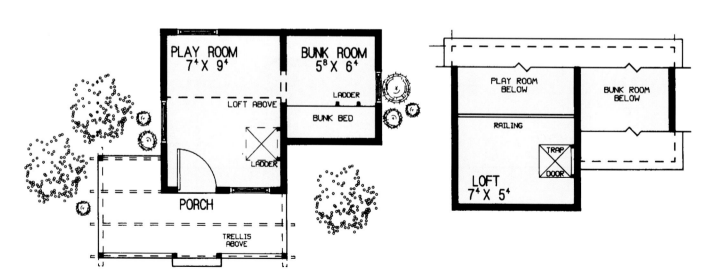

plan# HPT950061

Width: 8'-0"
Depth: 8'-0"

This Victorian playhouse can be the answer to a child's every dream. From the woodcut decorations to the box-bay windows—complete with hidden storage compartments— your children will enjoy hours of playtime in this petite house. Install a child-sized half-door and real windows, and paint the exterior in vivid colors and presto! You have a sturdy home that could even be around for your grandchildren. Inside, you can paint the walls with cartoon characters or even paint a faux fireplace on one wall. A vaulted ceiling gives a feeling of space, and the transom windows let sunlight flood in.

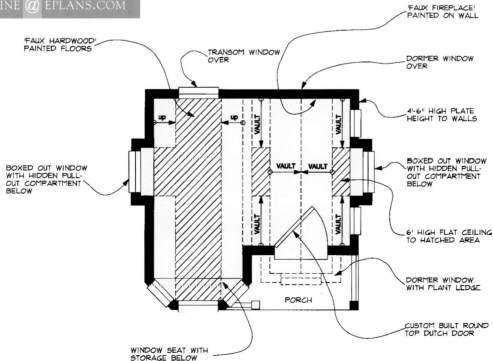

Lords and ladies, knights and evil-doers—this playhouse has everything except a fire-breathing dragon! Your children will spend hours re-enacting the days of kings and queens and knights of the Round Table. Surprisingly easy to build, this playset right out of King Arthur's Court uses standard materials. One corner of the playhouse holds a sandbox, and a stairway leads to a tower with its own catwalk. The area under the stairway could be enclosed to make a storage room for toys. The double castle doors can be fitted with standard hardware, but wrought-iron hinges will make this innovative playhouse look even more like a castle.

plan# **HPT950062**

Width: 11'-0"
Depth: 10'-0"

SEARCH ONLINE @ EPLANS.COM

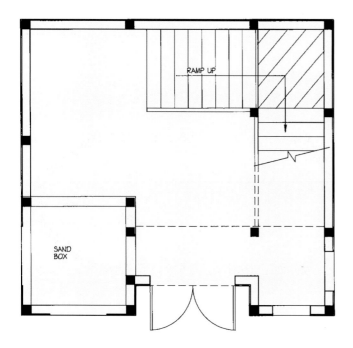

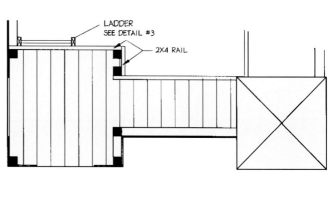

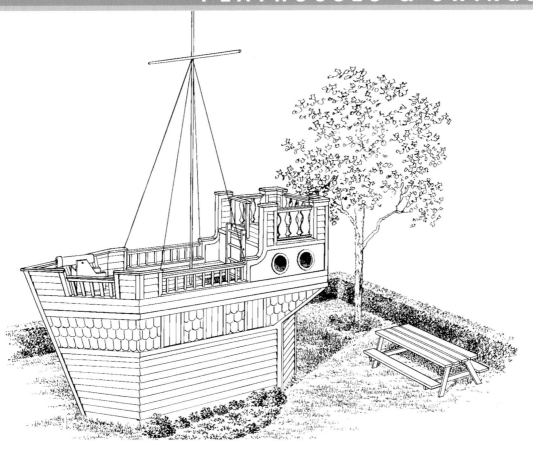

plan# HPT950063

When it comes to playhouses, it just doesn't get much better than this. Any child's imagination will sail over mysterious, unknown seas every time he or she enters this playhouse. More than 15 feet from stem to stern, this unique playhouse is easier to build than it looks. Constructed entirely of standard materials, the design includes a cannon on the main deck and gun ports in the hold that pull open to simulate a real Spanish galleon. A concrete foundation is recommended for this structure, due to its overall height—9'-5 1/2"—and the number of children who will be sailing off to wonderful places.

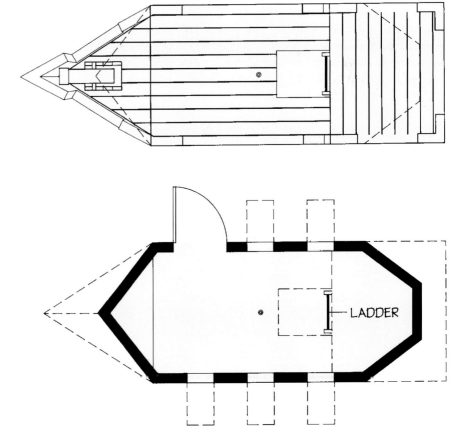

LADDER

A playhouse, a tree house, a lookout tower...your children will invent many uses for this mini-gazebo perched almost eight feet above the ground. It's large enough for a small table and chairs for a picnic or a Mad Hatter's tea party. Or, spread out some sleeping bags and invite friends for an overnight adventure—but no sleepwalking! The ladder, swings, and slide all add to the fun and can be modified to accommodate the ages of your children. If you have a full-size gazebo on your site, or plan to build one, you could use a similar design in the railings for both units for a surprising "double-take" effect.

plan# **HPT950064**

Width: 17'-0"
Depth: 11'-8"

SEARCH ONLINE @ EPLANS.COM

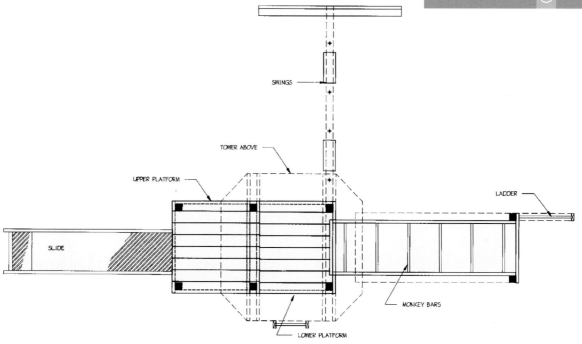

plan# HPT950065

A playset with a little bit of everything! This playset is designed to use any of the shelf-style swing units available at your local supplier. There are two slides—one regular, the other an enclosed spiral slide to provide added thrills. The ramp is designed for kids who like to climb back up the slide. Now they can climb up the ramp and slide down the other side. For small children, you can add a knotted rope to help them up. The climb to the Eagle's Nest will provide your kids with exercise for their muscles and their imagination. Young children will love to switch from one part of this playset to another, over and over again.

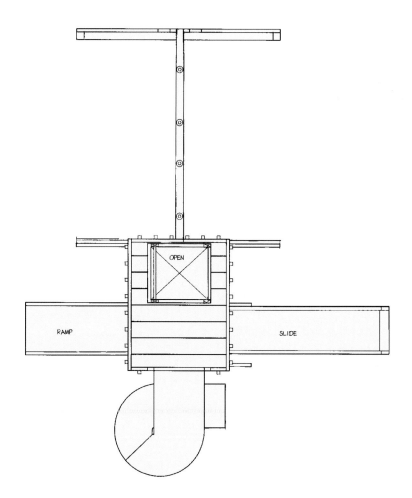

plan# **HPT950066**

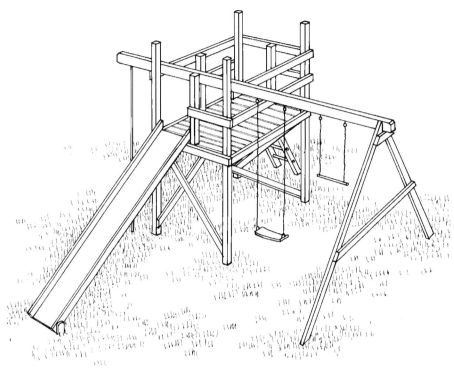

A backyard entertainment center for the kids! Build this multi-station playset and summertime fun is guaranteed. Containing two swings, a slide, and an upper deck that becomes, in the imagination, the deck of a boat, a lookout tower, or a lofty treehouse setting, this playset is great for all ages. Encourage your children to engage in active play—and exercise their young muscles. This project is simple to build from standard materials found at your nearest home center.

plan# **HPT950068**

This multilevel jungle gym enjoys platforms, which create a unique play structure. You can bring up some small chairs or tables and have a tea party, or you can spread out some sleeping bags and invite friends for an overnight adventure. The imagination of a child will find a pirate ship, a castle, or maybe Tarzan's tree house. In addition to the stairs, there is an even more fun and challenging way to climb up and down—a rope ladder!

The highlight of this delightful playset is the swinging bridge. It is available ready-made in a variety of styles or you can make it yourself. Designed for kids five and older, this playset includes a ladder inset at an angle to help developmental coordination. Both shelf-style swings and a popular tire swing are provided for variety. Hardware for the swings is available from your local suppliers. For larger tire swings, simply extend the support beam to accept a larger swing area. This playset is designed to sit on the ground; however, the firefighter's pole should be sunk into the ground six to eight inches to give it additional stability.

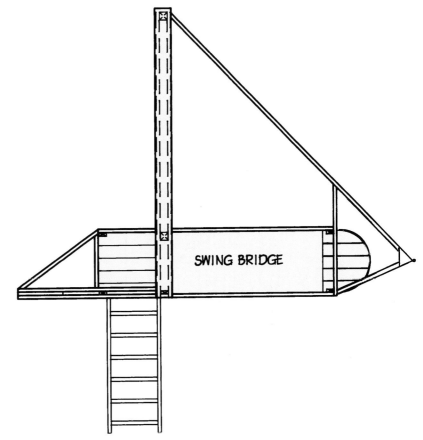

SWING BRIDGE

plan# HPT950112

Width: 8'-0"
Depth: 8'-0"

What youngster doesn't want a playhouse of his very own—where he can stretch his imagination to the limits? This delightful cottage is not only an engaging spot for your children to play, but it is a charming addition to your backyard or garden. With a covered front porch, a sunburst pediment over the door, window boxes, and shuttered windows, it's a miniature Victorian farmhouse to the last detail. When the kids have grown, it becomes the garden potting shed you've always wanted.

plan# HPT950113

Width: 8'-0"
Depth: 12'-0"

This quaint chalet design is like something you would find in a storybook. It can either be used as a playhouse for children or a storage shed for Mom and Dad—make it a playhouse in the summer and a storage shed in the off-season. The exterior is ornamented by a decorative window with shutters. The interior includes lots of space—choose a wood floor on concrete piers or a concrete floor.

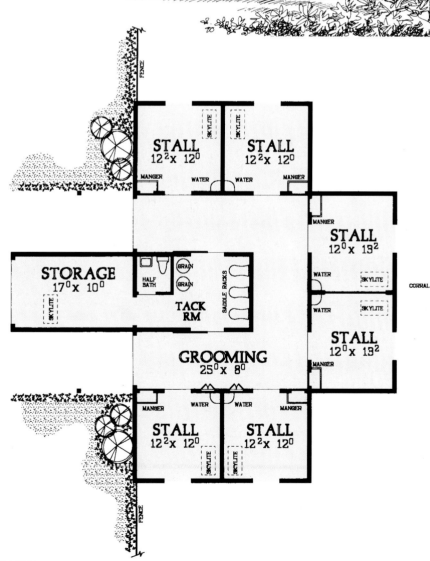

plan# HPT950069

Width: 56'-0"
Depth: 53'-0"

SEARCH ONLINE @ EPLANS.COM

If you run a large operation, consider this expanded floor plan for your stable requirements. Six 12'-2" x 12' livestock pens with dirt floors feature built-in feed and water troughs and Dutch doors leading either to a fenced exercise area or into either of two conveniently located grooming areas. Both grooming areas have grooved cement floors, sloped for easy hosing and draining. A convenient connecting hall between the grooming areas also has sloped concrete floors for easy maintenance. A central secured tack room with built-in saddle racks and grain bins, a bath with a toilet and sink, and a 10' x 17' inside storage area for hay complete the available features. Seven skylights throughout the structure provide an abundance of natural light.

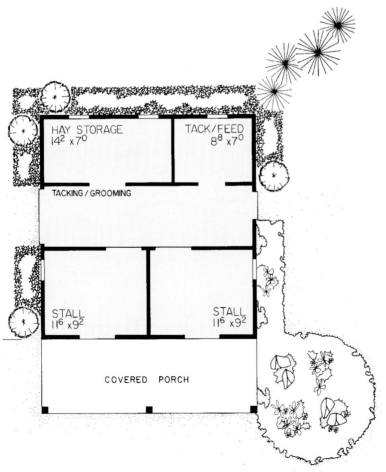

HAY STORAGE
14² x7⁰

TACK/FEED
8⁸ x7⁰

TACKING / GROOMING

STALL
11⁶ x9²

STALL
11⁶ x9²

COVERED PORCH

plan# **HPT950070**

Width: 24'-0"
Depth: 32'-0"

SEARCH ONLINE @ EPLANS.COM

Right out of Kentucky horse country comes this all-in-one design for a two-horse stable, plus tack room and covered hay storage. Two generous 11'-6" x 9'-2" stalls provide shelter and security for your best stock, with easy access through Dutch doors. Against the far wall is a 14'-2" x 7' hay "loft" and next to it, an 8'-8" x 7' tack room. In the center is a large area reserved for grooming your mount or to saddle up for the big race.

plan# HPT950071

Width: 26'-0"
Depth: 32'-0"

SEARCH ONLINE @ EPLANS.COM

This expanded structure will be home to your prize stock! Outside, a 26' x 12' covered area with a concrete floor provides storage and parking for tractors and other equipment. Inside, six skylights illuminate the interior of three areas: 1) two 12'-2" x 12' pens with dirt floors, each with built-in feed troughs, freshwater hookups and Dutch doors leading to an outdoor fenced area; 2) a covered grooming area with sloped, grooved concrete flooring and maximum access through double doors at each end; and 3) a 17' x 10' storage area with concrete floors for hay and a 7'-6" x 10' secured tack room with built-in saddle racks.

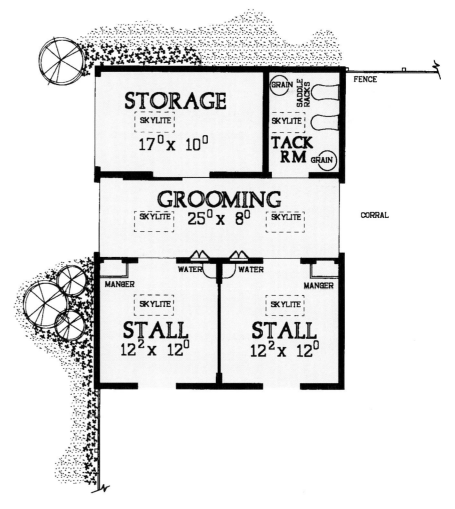

This large, sturdy lawn shed is not quite "as big as a barn," but almost! A combined area of 768 square feet—with 384 square feet per floor—includes a 24 'x 16' loft area with access by ladder or stairway. The structure is built entirely of standard framing materials requiring no special beams or cutting. An ideal hideaway for the serious artist, this structure could serve a myriad of other uses including a second garage, a game house, or even as a barn for small livestock. Or, expand the design to include utilities and a bathroom to provide a secluded guest room. The large tool room at the back has a built-in work bench with plenty of natural light, plus entrances from inside or outside. If your house has a fireplace, space is provided for a built-in wood stockpile area. The same space could be used to extend the length of the tool room. A louvered cupola and a 6' x 7' sliding-door entrance with crossbars accent the rural effect.

plan# **HPT950072**

Width: 24'-0"
Depth: 16'-0"

SEARCH ONLINE @ EPLANS.COM

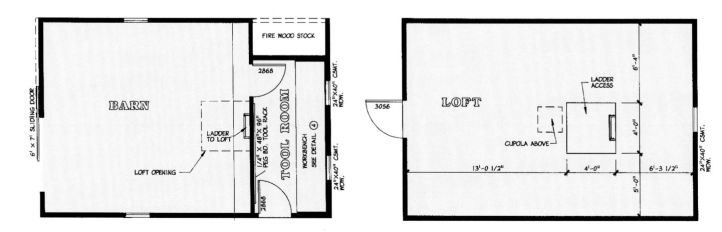

plan# HPT950073

Width: 26'-0"
Depth: 44'-0"

SEARCH ONLINE @ EPLANS.COM

With 832 square feet under its roof, this structure serves as a fine stable. Outside, a 26' x 12' covered area with a concrete floor provides storage and parking for tractors and other equipment. Inside, find stalls for two horses; these feature skylights, built-in feed troughs, and fresh water hookups. A centrally located grooming area, also brightened by skylights, opens to either side through Dutch doors. An indoor storage area and a full tack room—with built-in saddle racks—complete the structure.

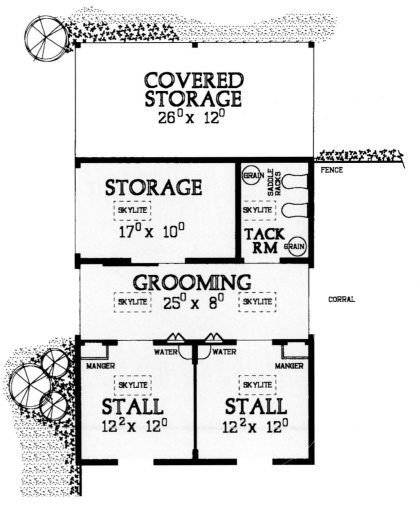

COVERED STORAGE
26^0 x 12^0

FENCE

STORAGE
SKYLITE
17^0 x 10^0

GRAIN
SADDLE RACKS

SKYLITE

TACK RM
GRAIN

GROOMING
SKYLITE 25^0 x 8^0 SKYLITE

CORRAL

WATER   WATER
MANGER   MANGER

STALL
SKYLITE
12^2 x 12^0

STALL
SKYLITE
12^2 x 12^0

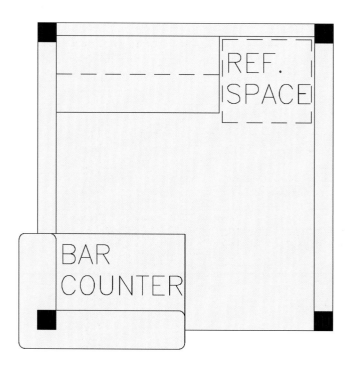

plan# **HPT950074**

Width: 8'-0"
Depth: 8'-0"

SEARCH ONLINE @ EPLANS.COM

This petite 64-square-foot pavilion design is perfect for private and refreshing entertaining. Build this structure close to a pool area to save trips in and out of the home kitchen. Summer leisure time can be more comfortably spent with this convenience close at hand. A refrigerator space is generously provided alongside a counter preparation area. Above, built-in shelves may be added for extra storage. On the opposite side, a bar counter resides for accessible convenience.

ORDER BLUEPRINTS 24 HOURS, 7 DAYS A WEEK, AT 1-800-521-6797

Here's a unique design that can be converted to serve a variety of functions: a tool shed, a barbecue stand, a pool-supply depot, or a sports-equipment locker. Apply a little imagination to come up with additional ways to use this versatile design to enhance your outdoor living space. As a tool shed, this design features a large potting bench with storage above and below. As a summer kitchen, it includes a built-in grill, a sink, and a refrigerator. For use as a pool-supply depot or equipment storage, it comes with a locker to store chemicals or valuable sports equipment safely. This structure is designed to be movable but, depending on its function, could be placed on a concrete slab.

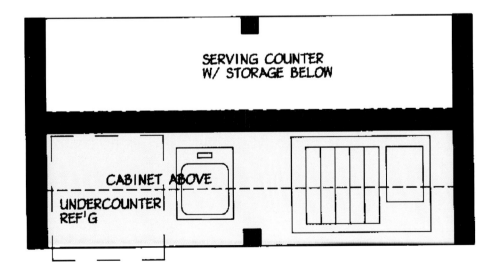

SERVING COUNTER
W/ STORAGE BELOW

CABINET ABOVE

UNDERCOUNTER
REF'G

This 218-square-foot cabana dream complements any poolside manor. A rustic blend of siding and cedar shingles graces the exterior and adds a stylish ornamentation to any private yard. A shaded, quaint covered porch welcomes you to three separate doors. To the right, a private changing chamber offers a bench and linen closet, and is illuminated by a single window. The center room provides a separate outdoor storage area—useful for large or bulky pool equipment such as rafts, games, or tubes. To the left, a private outdoor bathroom is a useful addition. This room is brightened by a window and features a sink, toilet, and separate shower for convenient use. This design can save dozens of trips in and out of the home, providing important efficiency to your private home pool scene.

plan# **HPT950076**

Width: 20'-0"
Depth: 12'-0"

SEARCH ONLINE @ EPLANS.COM

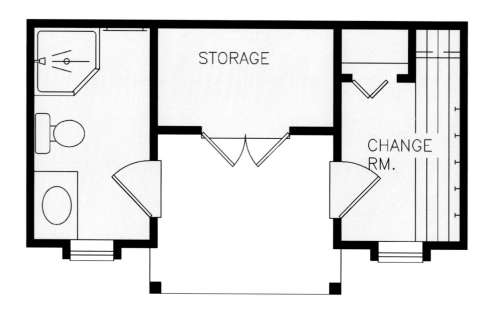

plan # **HPT950077**

Width: 12'-0"
Depth: 10'-0"

This 120-square-foot poolside cabana design has a cottage quaintness that will charm any scene. The wood siding and shingle exterior is enhanced by ornamental planter boxes—add bright flowers to decorate your leisurely summer retreat. Two windows naturally brighten the interior. The right side houses a changing room, which features a built-in wood bench and a convenient towel closet. The left room offers an outdoor bathroom, complete with a sink, toilet, and shower area. Practical and comfortable, this cabana easily provides every poolside need.

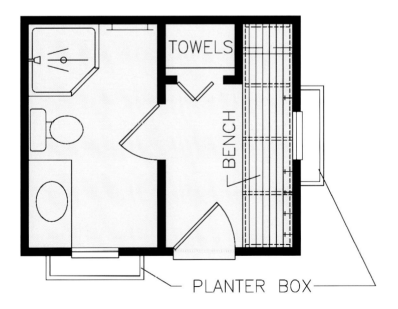

TOWELS

BENCH

PLANTER BOX

This stylish pavilion is an amusing outdoor retreat for any family. A hipped roof shades the inner area—keep a picnic table close by for outdoor barbecues and entertaining. To the right, a barbecue area is provided for outdoor grilling next to a convenient work counter—useful for preparing outdoor meals. A refrigerator space is also provided, next to another counter, for keeping cool foods fresh. The pavilion is completed by a bar counter, large enough to host a wide variety of refreshments. Decorate the outer perimeters with garden side plants. Built for the family that excels in entertaining, this structure is a lively addition to any property.

plan# **HPT950078**

Width: 16'-0"
Depth: 8'-0"

SEARCH ONLINE @ EPLANS.COM

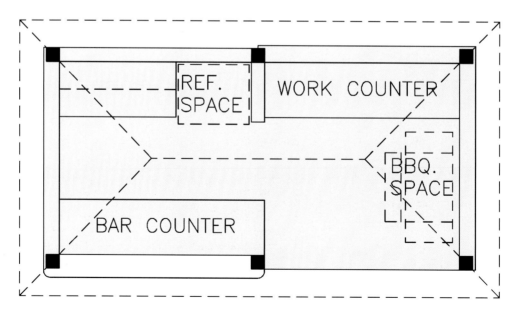

plan# HPT950079

Width: 24'-0"
Depth: 24'-0"

Entertain the possibilities for poolside parties with this smart, multifunctional ramada. Four corner units are united by open-air walkways and are almost literally tied together by a trellis roof. Pull up a chair to the outside bar in one corner for a refreshing drink or snack. Across the walkway is an efficiency kitchenette to make the goodies. In the next corner is a restroom and a shower, each with a separate entrance. The final corner hides all the pool essentials with double doors leading to the filter and pump room and a separate storage room for other pool equipment and toys.

QUOTE ONE®

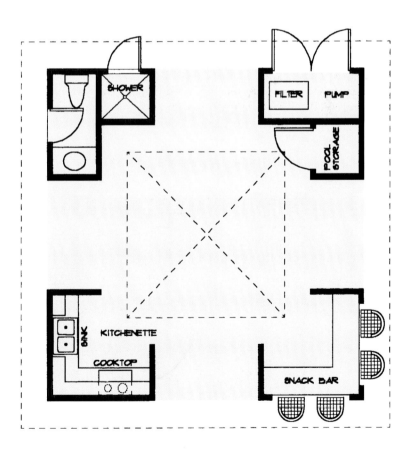

You can enhance both the beauty and the function of any pool area with this charming structure. A mini-kitchen and an optional built-in table are tucked in the breezeway of this double room; you'll have shelter for poolside repasts no matter what the weather. The exterior features include a gable roof with columns in the front, shuttered windows, horizontal wood and shingle siding, decorative flower boxes, and a cupola. The two rooms on either side of the breezeway area provide a 5'-8" x 7'-6" changing area with built-in seating and a larger area—7'-6" x 7'-6"—for convenient storage of pool supplies and equipment. This spacious cabana is sure to be a fine addition to an active family's pool area.

plan # **HPT950080**

Width: 24'-0"
Depth: 12'-8"

SEARCH ONLINE @ EPLANS.COM

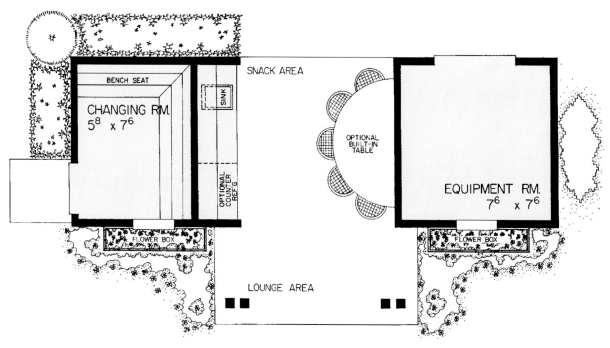

plan# HPT950081

Width: 47'-7"
Depth: 15'-4"

SEARCH ONLINE @ EPLANS.COM

The magic of this 728-square-foot design is its flexibility. Use it exclusively as a changing cabana with separate His and Hers changing rooms, or, with a little sleight of hand, turn one of the rooms into a summer kitchen for outdoor entertaining. As changing rooms, each eight-sided area includes built-in benches and private bathroom facilities. The kitchen option includes a stove, refrigerator, food-preparation area and a storage pantry. A shuttered window poolside provides easy access to serve your guests across the counter. Linking these two areas is a covered walkway which serves as a shaded picnic area or a convenient place to get out of the sun. Columns, arches, and stained-glass windows provide a touch of grandeur to this fun and functional poolside design.

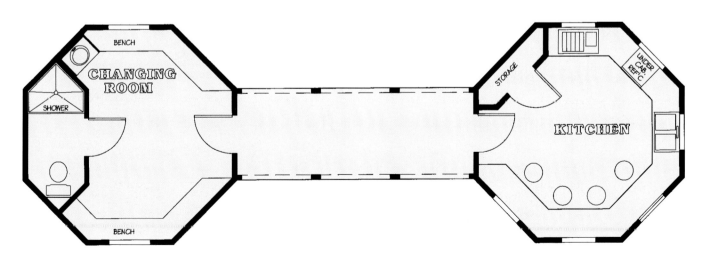

The family pet is offered their own private haven, in this deluxe-style dog house. This petite wooden structure is a necessity for the outdoor dog, and will blend well into any backyard setting. One exterior features an arched entrance and vertical wood siding. A second exterior is available and offers a more rectangular entrance with horizontal wood siding. Each presentation is designed to keep your dog cozy in any type of weather.

plan# **HPT950082**

Width: 3'-0"
Depth: 4'-0"

SEARCH ONLINE @ EPLANS.COM

ALTERNATE EXTERIOR

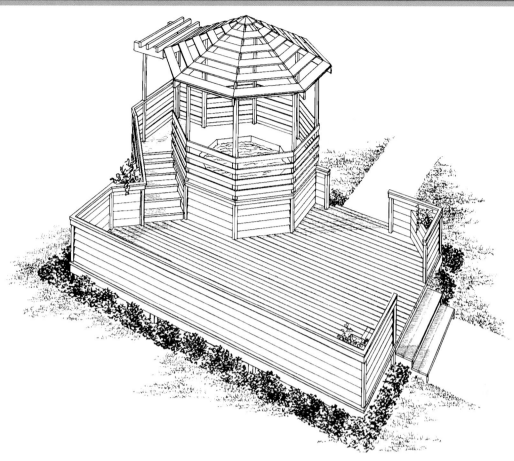

plan# HPT950083

Width: 24'-4"
Depth: 18'-10"

SEARCH ONLINE @ EPLANS.COM

Secluded enough for privacy, yet open enough to view the night sky through a curtain of vines on the trellis roof, this private outdoor spa has its own deck with built-in benches and planters. Approximately 280 square feet in area, the deck of this outstanding unit offers plenty of space to entertain friends and family. In the design shown, three steps lead up from the ground to the deck, and six additional steps lead up to the 7'x7' spa area. Patterned screens and a trellis roof provide privacy. You can place this spa adjacent to your house for convenient access, or install it as a free-standing unit in a secluded area of your property. Easy to build, this design will accommodate a spa of almost any style. The trellis roof can also be modified to a solid roof style or eliminated completely.

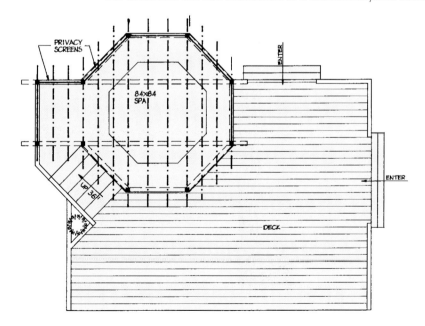

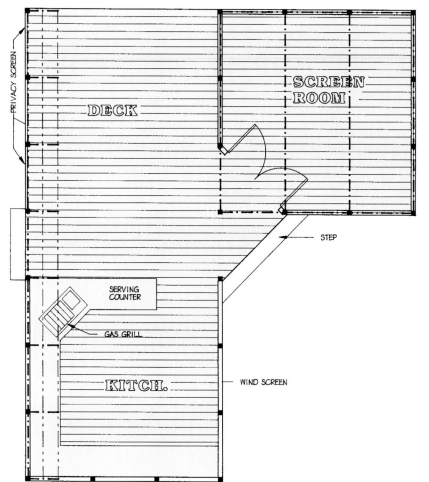

An outdoor kitchen and much, much more! For year-round, daylight-to-dark entertaining, consider this large outdoor entertainment unit. Nearly 700 square feet of floor space includes a deck for sun-bathing by day or dancing under the stars after sundown. A 13'x 13' -2" screened room provides a pest-free environment for cards or conversation. The Cookout Chef will rule with a flair over a full-service kitchen area that may include a grill, wet bar, sink, refrigerator, and ample room for storage. You can locate this versatile structure adjacent to your pool, or place it as a free-standing unit wherever your land-scape and site plan allow. Select material for the railings and privacy screens in patterns to match or complement your home.

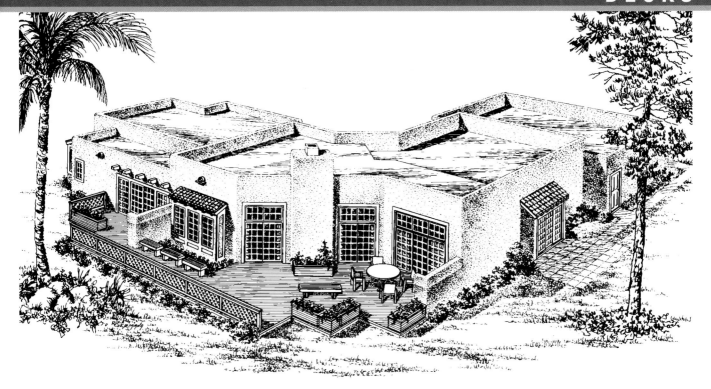

plan# **HPT950085**

SEARCH ONLINE @ EPLANS.COM

This is a deck of many surprises, all of which are artfully integrated into its design. A delightful, deck-level garden area, a private space off the master bedroom, and a unique treatment of movable planters combined with ground exits are just a few of the highlights.

The deck wraps around most of the rear of this home and encompasses over 850 square feet. The largest portion is accessed from the gathering room and dining room via three sets of sliding doors. There's plenty of space for table and chairs just outside the dining room. The deck sits on the ground level, so steps are not required to reach the backyard. Built-in planters are set at right angles to the two ground exits, giving the deck's perimeter an interesting jagged shape.

Though it is adaptable to any size or style of house, this deck was created to complement Home Planners Design HPB949. For more information about ordering blueprints for this home, call 1-800-521-6797.

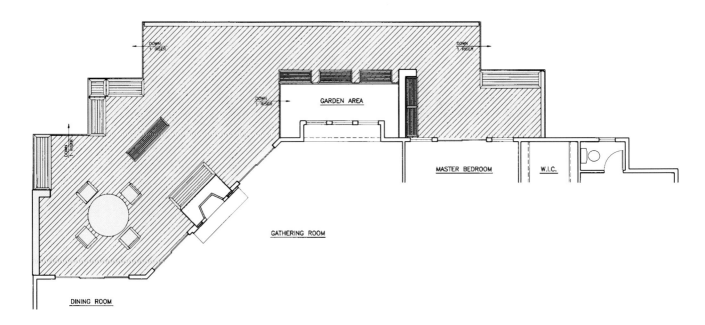

This deck is designed for an active family, as well as for entertaining. With two levels and two accesses from indoors, each area becomes a versatile extension of its adjacent room. The total deck area adds 945 square feet of outdoor living space. Both levels of this deck extend into the backyard. Stairway exits from level one and level two allow easy access to the ground from both the breakfast room and gathering room.

Built-in benches provide ample seating for guests. Though it is adaptable to any size or style of house, this deck was created to complement Home Planners Design HPB683. For information about ordering blueprints for this home, call 1-800-521-6797.

plan# **HPT950086**

SEARCH ONLINE @ EPLANS.COM

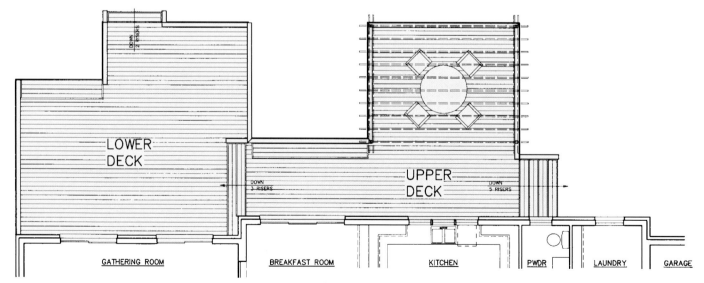

LOWER DECK

UPPER DECK

DOWN 2 RISERS

DOWN 3 RISERS

DOWN 5 RISERS

GATHERING ROOM   BREAKFAST ROOM   KITCHEN   PWDR   LAUNDRY   GARAGE

This deck is designed to be built as a simple, rectangular side deck, or to wrap around the corner of a home. Depending on the home's interior layout, it could be modified to allow access from two indoor rooms instead of one as shown here. The wrap design creates some interesting angles, which makes the deck seem much larger than its 445 square feet. Separate areas of the deck are natural settings for different activities. For example, the corner directly in front of the dining room door is more than adequate to accommodate a table and seating for four or more people. The opposite corner, away from the dining room, is an ideal place for built-in seating, as shown on this plan.

Though it is adaptable to any size or style of house, this deck was created to complement Home Planners Design HPB488. For information about ordering blueprints for this home, call 1-800-521-6797.

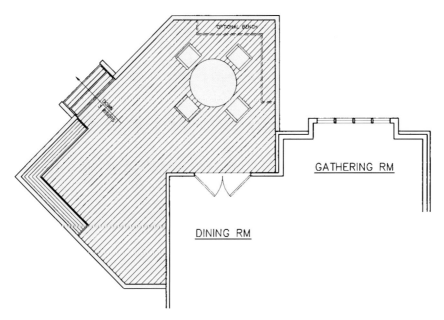

This deck, though not large, allows for an array of uses. Its geometric shape adds interest in a relatively small space—654 square feet. It also permits traffic to flow to and from the kitchen, making it convenient to wander to a deck-side table with a meal or a snack. The plan provides for a table and chairs to be tucked into the corner, just outside the breakfast-room entrance. A short wall (or optional handrail) here maintains privacy and protection. Continuous-level steps around the perimeter allow for complete access to the ground level.

Though it is adaptable to any size or style of house, this deck was created to complement Home Planners Design HPB855. For information about ordering blueprints for this home, call 1-800-521-6797.

plan# **HPT950088**

SEARCH ONLINE @ EPLANS.COM

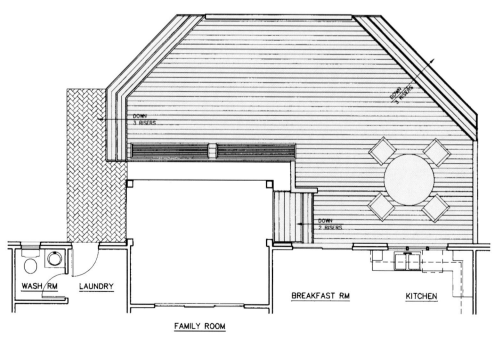

plan# HPT950089

SEARCH ONLINE @ EPLANS.COM

Looking for a total-living deck design? This plan, with its 1,700 square feet, wrap-around shape, and multiple accesses, suits any occasion. When a sunroom is included, this layout provides a variety of sun-to-shade conditions for almost every season. The sunroom, country kitchen, and additional room at the rear of the home provide access to the deck. Because so many rooms open to this expansive outdoor space, the possibilities to expand indoor activities—from casual kitchen gatherings to more elaborate entertaining—are numerous. Wrapping around the kitchen and sunroom, the deck spans nearly the entire rear of the house.

Though it is adaptable to any size or style of house, this deck was created to complement Home Planners Design HPB921. For information about ordering blueprints for this home, call 1-800-521-6797.

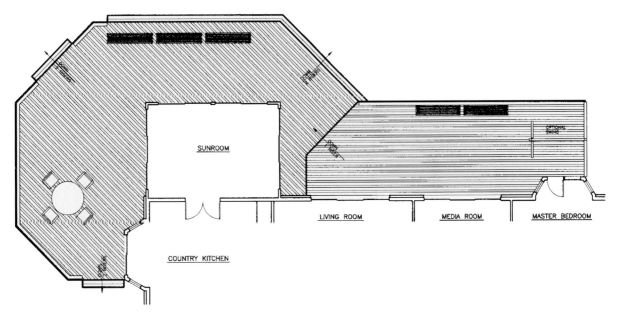

There is something special about spiral stairs. They are at once whimsical and practical. In this plan, a spiral staircase is utilized outdoors as a link between a private upstairs balcony and an expansive, first-floor deck. The appearance is dramatic, plus the staircase provides upstairs occupants quick and easy access to the deck below. This is a large deck, stretching twenty feet out from the home and extending forty feet wide for a total of over 800 square feet. The deck can be accessed from the first floor through both the gathering room and dining room. When combined, these rooms span thirty-one feet. When doors are opened to the outdoors, large groups can be accommodated with ease.

Though it is adaptable to any size or style of house, this deck was created to complement Home Planners Design HPB711. For information about ordering blueprints for this home, call 1-800-521-6797.

plan# **HPT950090**

SEARCH ONLINE @ EPLANS.COM

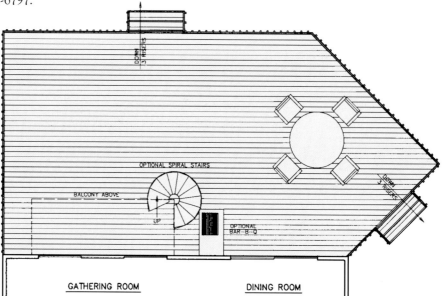

GATHERING ROOM   DINING ROOM

plan# HPT950091

SEARCH ONLINE @ EPLANS.COM

Much like a split-bedroom house plan, this is a split-deck design. One deck is more private, located outside the master bedroom. A section in the farthest left-hand deck is elevated to accommodate a whirlpool spa—an area that can be modified to suit manufacturer's specifications. Privacy screening repeats the same lines as this elevated section. In this instance, the screening is a simple construction of vertical boards, while built-in benches provide seating. Two steps down to the ground level, a brick walk serves as a guide to the family activities deck. The wide expanse between the two decks allows use of both simultaneously without interference between deck areas. This lower level functions as a separate outdoor room, with space for a table and chairs. A wet bar, tucked into a corner, helps reduce trips indoors for refreshments—a special touch to a highly appealing design. This 950-square-foot deck could be the perfect plan for summer or winter decking. Locate one deck in the shade, such as beneath a large tree; locate the other in a spot that will be bathed in plenty of winter sunshine. Though it is adaptable to any size or style of house, this deck was created to complement Home Planners Design HPB615. For more information about ordering blueprints for this home, call 1-800-521-6797.

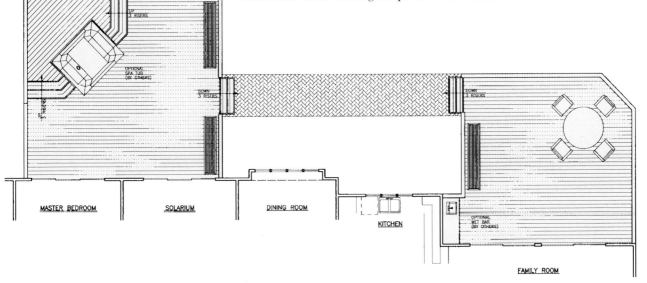

This long, rectangular deck is not only spacious (over 1,100 square feet), its shape allows separate activities to go on simultaneously without interference. Relax, play, catch a meal in the sun—it can all be done on this deck. Access from indoors to outdoors is accomplished by double doors on opposite sides of the gathering room and also from the breakfast room. This encourages the flow of traffic from indoors to outdoors—a real benefit for entertaining or for large families with various interests. A special feature of this deck is the screening that surrounds its perimeter. This is a valuable privacy addition for homes with small lots and nearby neighbors.

Though it is adaptable to any size or style of house, this deck was created to complement Home Planners Design HPB543. For information about ordering blueprints for this home, call 1-800-521-6797.

plan# **HPT950092**

SEARCH ONLINE @ EPLANS.COM

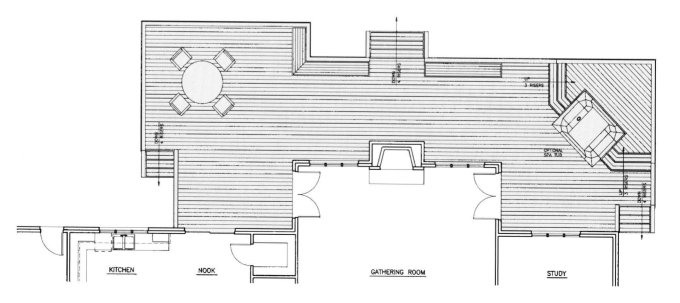

KITCHEN   NOOK   GATHERING ROOM   STUDY

Dramatic—in a big way—describes this deck design. This is a multi-purpose addition that also offers some very specialized features. First, it is an excellent choice for a hillside or slope—it is elevated well above the ground level to accommodate a steep slope or a rugged, rocky surface. Second, if the building lot is flat, it is simple to add a patio below—the upper portion of the deck provides shade from above. Sun, shade, and protection from the weather are available just about any time. If a lower-level patio is not desired, the area beneath the deck could be converted to a large storage area.

Because this spacious deck, with its 950 square feet of space, wraps around the entire rear of the house, it has access from the dining room, gathering room, and study. Though it is adaptable to any size or style of house, this deck was created to complement Home Planners Design HPB511. For information about ordering blueprints for this home, call 1-800-521-6797.

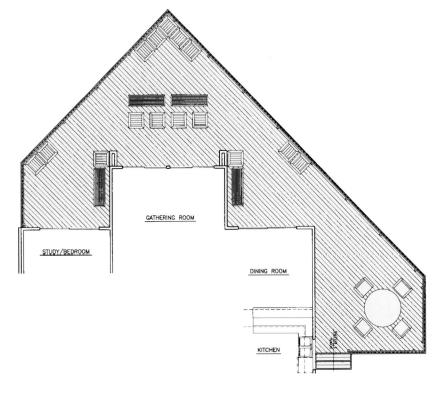

What a spectacular deck—sure to elicit admiration from all who see it! Designed to be absolutely spacious, with over 1,400 square feet, this deck features two levels—an upper level and a ground level. A railed staircase links the two levels for convenience. The upper level is a natural for entertaining. It is actually three connected decks and can be reached by several rooms—all with sliding doors. Deck surface patterns change from area to area, reinforcing the feeling of multiple outdoor rooms. The ground level is designed more for privacy, featuring screening and a secluded spa.

Though it is adaptable to any size or style of house, this deck was created to complement Home Planners Design HPB934. For more information about ordering blueprints for this home, call 1-800-521-6797.

plan# **HPT950094**

SEARCH ONLINE @ EPLANS.COM

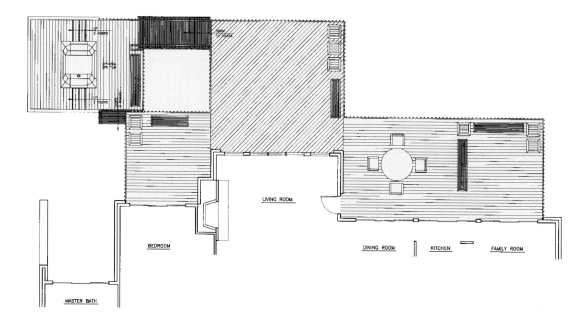

LIVING ROOM

BEDROOM

DINING ROOM   KITCHEN   FAMILY ROOM

MASTER BATH

This is an unusual design that will suit a special home and owners who have a flair for the provocative. It is particularly well-suited to homes with deep, narrow lots. The deck generates excitement from a striking octagonal shape and by a walkway that connects it to the house. This elevated walkway begins at a covered porch attached to the house; matching stairs on opposite sides of the walk provide access to ground level. Built-in seating is extensive—benches wrap around one entire section, covering three of the deck's eight sides.

Use this 700-square-foot design to create a totally different outdoor space separate from the home, so that stepping away from the covered porch is like stepping into another environment. The unusual shape allows for creative use of plants and trees near the deck to provide shade and seclusion.

Though it is adaptable to any size or style of house, this deck was created to complement Home Planners Design HPB969. For more information about ordering blueprints for this home, call 1-800-521-6797.

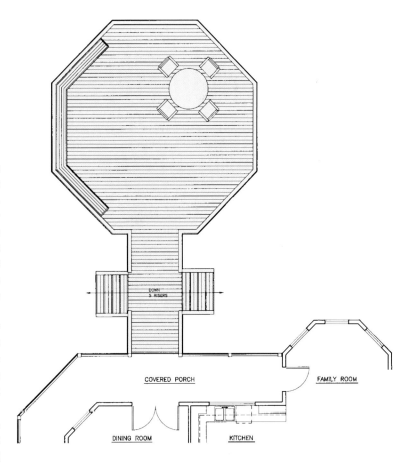

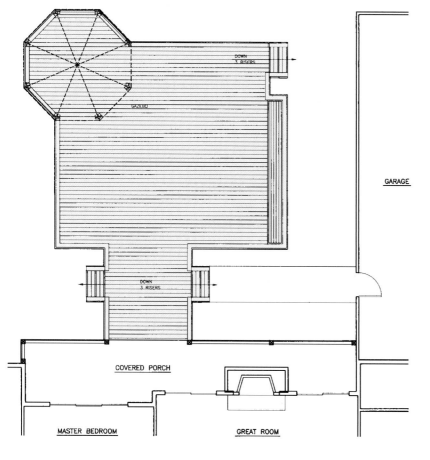

GARAGE

DOWN
3 RISERS

GAZEBO

DOWN
3 RISERS

COVERED PORCH

MASTER BEDROOM

GREAT ROOM

plan# HPT950096

Width: 31'-6"
Depth: 35'-6"

SEARCH ONLINE @ EPLANS.COM

This creative, 19th-Century deck is designed to provide interest and intrigue to any backyard landscape. It is sure to draw people from indoors to out—inviting exploration of its 800 square feet of deck area and the dramatic octagonal gazebo.

Designed with entertaining in mind, the deck features a built-in bench that runs along the entire length of one side. The tall peaked gazebo extends the deck outward—an interesting focal point when viewed from indoors or from the covered porch. The gazebo also provides cooling shade and is just the right size for a table and chairs.

Though it is adaptable to any size or style of house, this deck was created to complement Home Planners Design HPB953. For more information about ordering blueprints for this home, call 1-800-521-6797.

Long and angular are two words that help describe this elevated, easy-to-install deck. The 750-square-foot design is contained in a single level, but the many changes in angles along the perimeter provide interest. The deck can be reached from indoors via the dining room and the master bedroom. The deck area outside the dining room extends farther out from the house, creating a perfect spot for setting up a table and chairs for open-air dining or relaxing. Sliding doors from the master bedroom take you out onto a narrower, rectangular section of the deck, which is somewhat separate from the dining area.

Benches follow the angles of the perimeter, and are protected with a railing. Two stairways—one near the dining alcove, the other across from the master-bedroom doorway—provide access to the ground level. Though it is adaptable to any size or style of house, this deck was created to complement Home Planners Design HPB941. For more information about ordering blueprints for this home, call 1-800-521-6797.

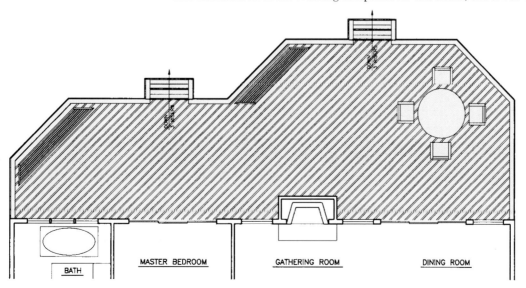

BATH

MASTER BEDROOM   GATHERING ROOM   DINING ROOM

Spanning nearly the entire width of the home, this 950-square-foot deck can be accessed from several rooms. The area off the master bedroom is the perfect location for a semi-private gathering spot. Doors from the gathering room open onto the center of the deck. And, perhaps most convenient of all, the deck can be quickly reached from the dining room, for alfresco dining on the outdoor table and chairs. Visually, the deck provides impact with its angular chevron or delta design—the most acute angles create an interesting scene from the gathering-room window. Built-in benches "V" together for dramatic outdoor seating. Matching stairways on opposite sides of the benches provide dual access to ground level. Another utilitarian feature of this deck is the garage access, near the chair and seating corner. Moving items to and from the deck for use and storage couldn't be easier. Though it is adaptable to any size or style of house, this deck was created to complement Home Planners Design HPB505. For more information about ordering blueprints for this home, call 1-800-521-6797.

plan# **HPT950098**

Width: 57'-4"
Depth: 30'-4"

SEARCH ONLINE @ EPLANS.COM

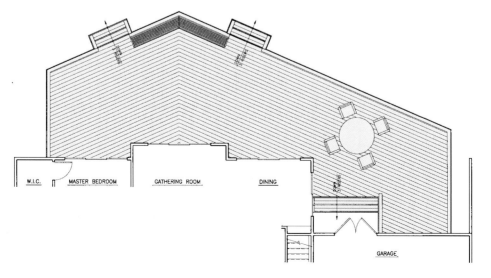

W.I.C.   MASTER BEDROOM   GATHERING ROOM   DINING

GARAGE

plan# **HPT950099**

SEARCH ONLINE @ EPLANS.COM

Simple, yet possessing interesting design features, this center-view deck would be a valuable and functional addition to any home. Its broad, compact shape provides ample space for gatherings, meals, and family activities in over 750 square feet. The deck can be accessed from both the dining room and family room. Special features include space for bay-window pop-outs in the nook between these two rooms. The windows project onto the deck area—providing interesting angles indoors and out. Access to the ground is reached via two stairways—one is located front and center, flanked by two raised planter boxes, which will help guide foot traffic to the stair entrance. Another stairway is located nearest the family room, providing quick accessibility to the adjacent mudroom. Railings surround the perimeter for safety. Though it is adaptable to any size or style of house, this deck was created to complement Home Planners Design HPB610. For more information about ordering blueprints for this home, call 1-800-521-6797.

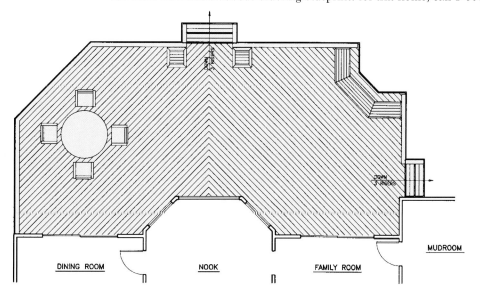

DINING ROOM   NOOK   FAMILY ROOM

MUDROOM

Although not a large expanse, just over 525 square feet, this stylish deck makes use of angles and strategic placement to create a sense of spaciousness and room extension. Indoors, a large country kitchen features dual sliding doors opening onto the deck, making the kitchen more accessible to the outdoors. This design is also distinguished by its contemporary wedge shape, and could be a problem-solving design for a small or odd-shaped lot. Built-in benches provide extensive seating—enough for fairly large gatherings. The railing is bolstered by privacy-creating latticework. One set of intricately designed stairs veers outward to ground level, helping guide users, and provides a custom touch to this simple yet highly functional deck. Though it is adaptable to any size or style of house, this deck was created to complement Home Planners Design HPB682. For information about ordering blueprints for this home, call 1-800-521-6797.

plan# **HPT950100**

SEARCH ONLINE @ EPLANS.COM

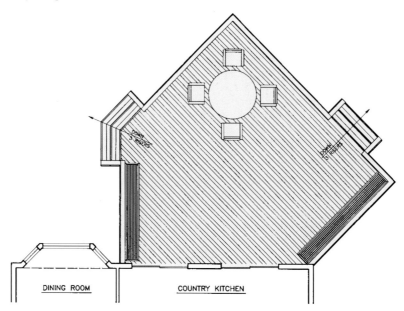

DINING ROOM   COUNTRY KITCHEN

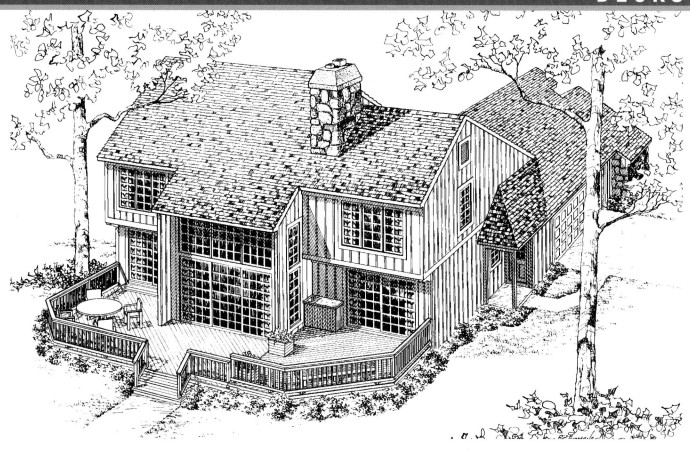

The broad U-shaped design of this bi-level deck places it in the out-of-the-ordinary category. Wrapping around three rooms, the 600-square-foot deck allows multiple views and access. A unique aspect of this deck is the creation of two separate deck spaces. The separation of these two areas is reinforced by using distinctly different decking surface patterns. This deck also has some custom amenities to make outdoor entertaining a breeze. A wet bar is tucked into a corner created by the adjoining study and gathering room. A built-in bench is aligned with one side of the deck's perimeter, located just outside of the study. Spacious yet intimate, the deck features plenty of room outside of the dining room for a table and chairs, providing a convenient place to relax and enjoy meals. Stairs to the ground level and a safety railing around the perimeter complete this picture-perfect design. Though it is adaptable to any size or style of house, this deck was created to complement Home Planners Design HPB826. For more information about ordering blueprints for this home, call 1-800-521-6797.

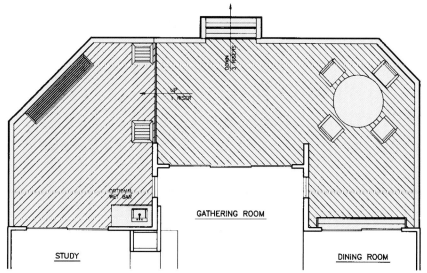

This spilt-level deck is a pleasing combination of rectangular and octagonal shapes. The result is a functional and highly attractive outdoor living space of over 625 square feet. The two-level design helps promote a two-decks-in-one feeling. In addition, each level can be accessed by separate indoor rooms.

Level one features an octagonal extension, blossoming from one corner of the rectangular section. The octagonal shape is perfect for accommodating a table and chairs. Handily, this area is located just outside of the dining room and kitchen. Stairs near the center of the rectangle lead to the ground. The second level is a single step down from level one. This area has separate access from the family room. Three built-in benches provide plenty of seating for family activities and entertaining. Permanent square-shaped planters flank the stairs, helping identify the stairway and move traffic around safely. Though it is adaptable to any size or style of house, this deck was created to complement Home Planners Design HPA956. For information about ordering blueprints for this home, call 1-800-521-6797.

plan# **HPT950102**

SEARCH ONLINE @ EPLANS.COM

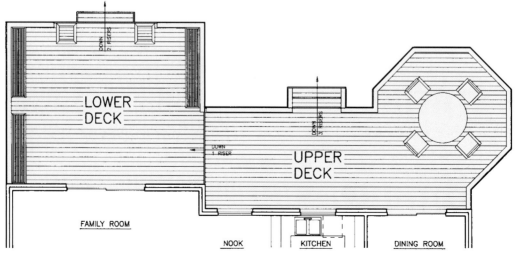

plan# HPT950103

SEARCH ONLINE @ EPLANS.COM

This rectangular-shaped deck is long and spacious—over 800 square feet, perfect for entertaining. In this instance, it adjoins a covered porch—a real advantage in certain regions when the weather does not cooperate. Multiple access—from the master bedroom, gathering room and dining room—helps ensure this deck's utility. A table-and-chairs setting is positioned near the dining room to make it convenient to serve outdoor meals.

The stairway is built wide in a striking V design. Additional custom features include built-in benches and planters. Railings surround the perimeter of the decking for safety. In this example, latticework has been added to the railing for the enhanced feeling of privacy and enclosure. Though it is adaptable to any size or style of house, this deck was created to complement Home Planners Design HPB802. For more information about ordering blueprints for this home, call 1-800-521-6797.

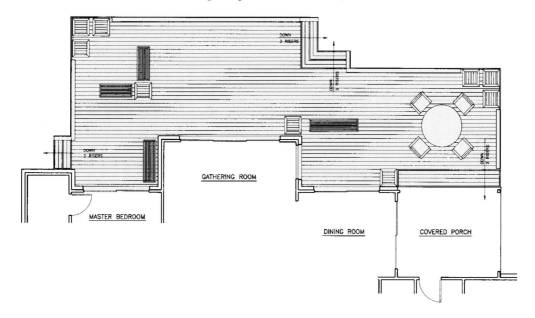

DOWN
3 RISERS

DOWN
2 RISERS

GATHERING ROOM

MASTER BEDROOM

DINING ROOM

COVERED PORCH

With three levels totaling over 650 square feet and an elongated shape, this deck is well-suited for simultaneous activities without disturbing the participating parties. Because the deck areas are linked and easy to reach, it is also excellent for large gatherings. Stairways are not required to go from one level to the next—the deck is thoughtfully designed so that each level has a change in elevation equal to a step. The result is a deck composed of three separate areas, made even more distinctive by contrasting surface patterns for each area.

In addition to the expansive bench seating, a moveable grill is installed near the kitchen door for barbecues. The grill can also be built as a wet bar. Planters add a finishing touch. Though it is adaptable to any size or style of house, this deck was created to complement Home Planners Design HPB356. For information about ordering blueprints for this home, call 1-800-521-6797.

plan# **HPT950104**

SEARCH ONLINE @ EPLANS.COM

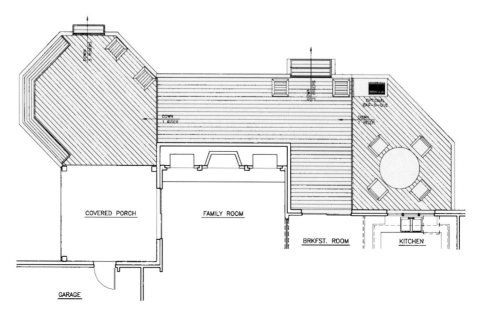

COVERED PORCH · FAMILY ROOM · BRKFST. ROOM · KITCHEN · GARAGE

plan ⊕ **HPT950105**

SEARCH ONLINE @ EPLANS.COM

A contemporary design is just one attribute of this diminutive yet appealing deck. An overall feeling of spaciousness is achieved in a small area (550 square feet) due to the creative changes in angle and space. This design would work extremely well on an odd-shaped lot, or where existing trees or other landscape features require some ingenuity and imagination to achieve a good "fit." Benches are built between matching planters in an area outside of the living room for an intimate seating arrangement.

The deck extends outward dramatically to create a large area outside of the family room, with plenty of space for a table and chairs. Railings surround the deck for a finishing touch, as well as for safety. A simple single step down provides access to ground level in three different corners of the deck. Though it is adaptable to any size or style of house, this deck was created to complement Home Planners Design HPB379. For information about ordering blueprints for this home, call 1-800-521-6797.

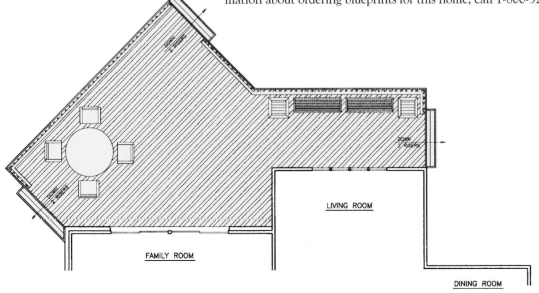

LIVING ROOM

FAMILY ROOM

DINING ROOM

This is an exciting, symmetrical deck of over 1,500 square feet that invites exploration. It is a perfect deck for a site blessed with a view—the deck angles command the eye outside and away toward the horizon. Three levels and three accesses—from the study, gathering room, and master bedroom—make this a highly versatile and usable deck. It can be utilized as three private decks or one extremely spacious deck. The centered V-shaped section, reached by twin sliding doors from the gathering room, is on a level two steps down from smaller matching decks on opposite sides.

Though it is adaptable to any size or style of house, this deck was created to complement Home Planners Design HPB781. For more information about ordering blueprints for this home, call 1-800-521-6797.

plan # **HPT950106**

SEARCH ONLINE @ EPLANS.COM

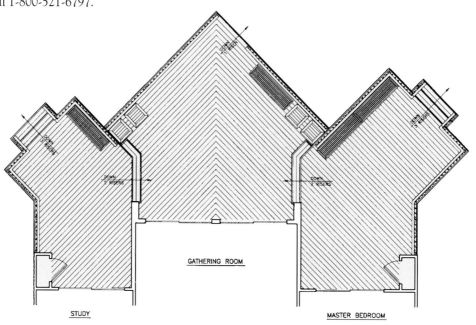

plan# **HPT950107**

SEARCH ONLINE @ EPLANS.COM

The split-level design of this deck is the perfect complement to the split-level house plan and even enhances its dramatic style. With a square footage of over 1,100, it allows two activities to go on simultaneously in almost complete privacy because the deck areas are separate and distinct. The main deck level can be reached by twin sliding doors from the family room or from an additional set of sliding doors in the breakfast room.

A railed stairway with seven steps takes you to the second deck, which can also be reached from the teenage activities room. Built-in planters and a pair of benches help make this deck cozy. Access to ground level is simple with two exits—one near the stairway to the main deck; the second heading toward a side yard. Though it is adaptable to any size or style of house, this deck was created to complement Home Planners Design HPB850. For information about ordering blueprints for this home, call 1-800-521-6797.

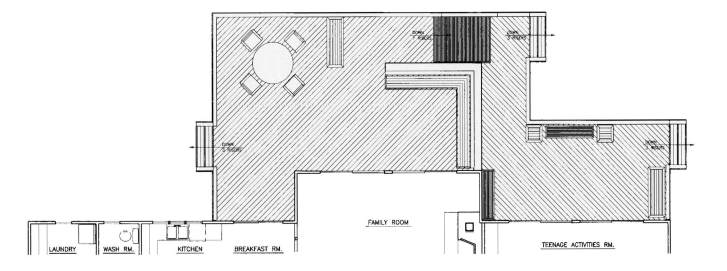

COPYRIGHT DOS & DON'TS

Blueprints for residential construction (or working drawings, as they are often called in the industry) are copyrighted intellectual property, protected under the terms of United States Copyright Law and, therefore, cannot be copied legally for use in building. However, we've made it easy for you to get what you need to build your home, without violating copyright law. Following are some guidelines to help you obtain the right number of copies for your chosen blueprint design.

COPYRIGHT DO

▧ Do purchase enough copies of the blueprints to satisfy building requirements. As a rule for a home or project plan, you will need a set for yourself, two or three for your builder and subcontractors, two for the local building department, and one to three for your mortgage lender. You may want to check with your local building department or your builder to see how many they need before you purchase. You may need to buy eight to 10 sets; note that some areas of the country require purchase of vellums (also called reproducibles) instead of blueprints. Vellums can be written on and changed more easily than blueprints. Also, remember, plans are only good for one-time construction.

▧ Do consider reverse blueprints if you want to flop the plan. Lettering and numbering will appear backward, but the reversed sets will help you and your builder better visualize the design.

▧ Do take advantage of multiple-set discounts at the time you place your order. Usually, purchasing additional sets after you receive your initial order is not as cost-effective.

▧ Do take advantage of vellums. Though they are a little more expensive, they can be changed, copied, and used for one-time construction of a home. You will receive a copyright release letter with your vellums that will allow you to have them copied.

▧ Do talk with one of our professional service representatives before placing your order. They can give you great advice about what packages are available for your chosen design and what will work best for your particular situation.

COPYRIGHT DON'T

▧ Don't think you should purchase only one set of blueprints for a building project. One is fine if you want to study the plan closely, but will not be enough for actual building.

▧ Don't expect your builder or a copy center to make copies of standard blueprints. They cannot legally—most copy centers are aware of this.

▧ Don't purchase standard blueprints if you know you'll want to make changes to the plans; vellums are a better value.

▧ Don't use blueprints or vellums more than one time. Additional fees apply if you want to build more than one time from a set of drawings. ■

THE DECK BLUEPRINT PACKAGE

OUR PLANS AND DETAILS ARE CAREFULLY PREPARED

in an easy-to-understand format that will guide you through every stage of your deck-building project. The Deck Blueprint Package contains four sheets outlining information pertinent to the specific Deck Plan you have chosen. A separate package—Deck Construction Details—provides the how-to data for building any deck, including instructions for adaptations and conversions.

DECK CONSTRUCTION DETAILS

In five information-packed sheets, these standard details provide all the general data necessary for building, adapting and converting any deck. Included are layout examples, framing patterns and foundation variation; details for ledgers, columns and beams; schedules and charts; handrail, stair and ramp details; and special options like spa platforms, planters, bars, benches and overhead trellises. This is a must-have package for the first-time deck builder and a useful addition to the custom deck plans.

Or buy the Complete Construction Set that includes plans for the Deck of your choice plus the Deck Construction Details—see blueprint price schedule for ordering information.

CUSTOM DECK PLANS

Each deck plan has been custom-designed by a professional architect.
With each Custom Deck Plan you receive the following:

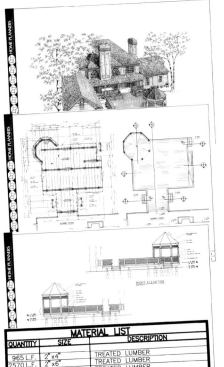

DECK PLAN FRONTAL SHEET

An artist's line drawing shows the deck as it connects to its matching or corresponding house. This drawing provides a visual image of what the deck will look like when completed, highlighting the livability factors.

DECK FRAMING AND FLOOR PLANS

In clear, easy-to-read drawings, this sheet shows all component parts of the deck from an aerial viewpoint with dimensions, notes and references. Drawn at 1/4"=1'-0", the floor plan provides a finished overhead view of the deck including rails, stairs, benches and ramps. The framing plan gives complete details on how the deck is to be built, including the position and spacing of footings, joists, beams, posts and decking materials. Where necessary, the sheet also includes sections and close-ups to further explain structural details.

DECK ELEVATIONS

Large-scale front and side elevations of the deck complete the visual picture of the deck. Drawn at 3/8"=1'-0", the elevations show the height of rails, balusters, stair risers, benches and other deck accessories.

DECK MATERIALS LIST

This is a complete shopping list of all the materials needed (including sizes and amounts) to build your deck. The Materials List is complemented by section drawings showing placement of hardware such as thru-bolts, screws, nuts, washers and nails and how these items are used to secure deck flooring, rails, posts and joists.

YARD & GARDEN STRUCTURES BLUEPRINT PACKAGE

THE BLUEPRINT PACKAGE FOR THESE INSPIRING YARD AND GARDEN
structures contains everything you need to plan and build the outdoor amenity of your choice. Some of the more complicated gazebos and lawn-shed packages will have several sheets to thoroughly explain how the structure will go together. The simpler structures such as bridges and arbors have fewer sheets. To help you further understand the process of constructing an outdoor structure, we also offer a separate package—Gazebo Construction Details—that outlines general information for construction of gazebos and similar outdoor amenities. Included are numerous illustrations, an explanation of building terms and general tips and hints to make your building project progress smoothly.

GAZEBO CONSTRUCTION DETAILS

This set of 24"x18" sheets contains a wealth of valuable information for gazebos and other outdoor building projects. Included are the steps of the building process; an explanation of terms; details for locating footings, piers and foundations; information about attaching posts to piers or footings; creating free-standing benches; and much, much more. These sheets will facilitate many different outdoor construction projects for the do-it-yourselfer and will make working with contractors and subcontractors more comfortable.

Or buy the Complete Construction Set that includes plans for the Yard or Garden Structure of your choice plus the Gazebo Construction Details—see blueprint price schedule for ordering informaiton.

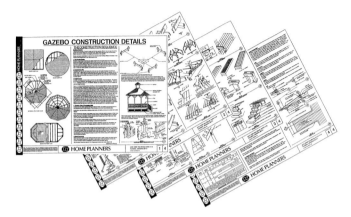

PROJECT STRUCTURE PLANS

The plans for our Yard and Garden Structures have been custom-created by a professional designer. Among the helpful sheets for building your structure may be such information as:

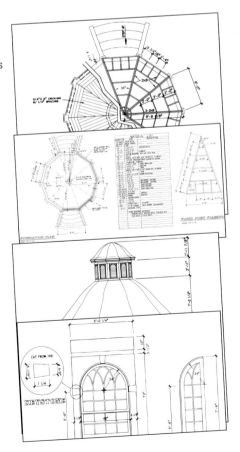

FLOOR PLAN

Done in ½"=1'-0" scale, this sheet shows the exact floor plan of the structure with dimensions, flooring patterns and window and door call-outs. Details found on other sheets may also be referenced on this sheet.

FOUNDATION AND JOIST DETAILS/MATERIALS LIST

This schematic of the foundation and floor and rafter joists, done in ¼"=1'-0" or ½"=1'-0" scale, gives dimensions and shows how to pour or construct the foundation and flooring components. The materials list is invaluable for estimating and planning work and acts as an accurate "shopping list" for the do-it-yourselfer.

ELEVATIONS AND FRAMING PLANS/WALL SECTIONS

Shown in ¼"=1'-0" or ½"=1'-0" scale, these helpful drawings show various views of the structure plus a complete framing plan for the flooring. Wall sections provide stud sizes, connector types, and rafter and roofing materials. They may also show mouldings or other trim pieces.

DETAILS

Cut-out details, shown in ¼"=1'-0" or 1"=1'-0" scale, are given for items such as pilaster framing, doors, side panels and rafter profiles. These details provide additional information and enhance your understanding of other aspects of the plans.

PRICE SCHEDULE & INDEX

BLUEPRINT PRICE SCHEDULE

TIERS	1-SET STUDY PACKAGE	4-SET BUILDING PACKAGE	8-SET BUILDING PACKAGE	1-SET REPRODUCIBLE*
P1	$20	$50	$90	$140
P2	$40	$70	$110	$160
P3	$70	$100	$140	$190
P4	$100	$130	$170	$220
P5	$140	$170	$210	$270
P6	$180	$210	$250	$310
A1	$440	$490	$540	$660

Requires a fax number

OPTIONS FOR PLANS IN TIERS A1
Additional Identical Blueprints
in same order for "A1" price plans ....**$50 per set**
Reverse Blueprints (mirror image) with 4- or 8-set order for "A1" plans ....**$50 fee per order**
Specification Outlines ....**$10 each**

IMPORTANT NOTES
• The 1-set study package is marked "not for construction."
• Prices for 4- or 8-set Building Packages honored only at time of original order.
• Additional identical blueprints may be purchased within 60 days of original order.

OPTIONS FOR PLANS IN TIERS P1–P6
Additional Identical Blueprints in same order for "P1–P6" price plans ....**$10 per set**
Reverse Blueprints (mirror image) for "P1–P6" price plans ....**$10 fee per order**
1 Set of Deck or Gazebo Construction Details ....**$14.95 each**
Deck or Gazebo Construction Package ....**add $10 to Building Package price**
(includes 1 set of "P1–P6" plans, plus 1 set Standard Gazebo Construction Details)

PLAN INDEX

OUR EXCHANGE POLICY

With the exception of reproducible plan orders, we will exchange your entire first order for an equal or greater number of blueprints within our plan collection within 90 days of the original order. The entire content of your original order must be returned before an exchange will be processed. Please call our customer service department for your return authorization number and shipping instructions. If the returned blueprints look used, redlined or copied, we will not honor your exchange. Fees for exchanging your blueprints are as follows: 20% of the amount of the original order...plus the difference in cost if exchanging for a design in a higher price bracket or less the difference in cost if exchanging for a design in a lower price bracket. **(Reproducible blueprints are not exchangeable or refundable.)** Please call for current postage and handling prices. Shipping and handling charges are not refundable. Please call our customer service department for your return authorization number and shipping instructions.

ABOUT REPRODUCIBLES

When purchasing a reproducible you may be required to furnish a fax number. The designer will fax documents that you must sign and return to them before shipping will take place.

ABOUT REVERSE BLUEPRINTS

Although lettering and dimensions will appear backward, reverses will be a useful aid if you decide to flop the plan. See Price Schedule and Plans Index for pricing.

REVISING, MODIFYING AND CUSTOMIZING PLANS

Like many homeowners who buy these plans, you and your builder, architect or engineer may want to make changes to them. We recommend purchase of a reproducible plan for any changes made by your builder, licensed architect or engineer. As set forth below, we cannot assume any responsibility for blueprints which have been changed, whether by you, your builder or by professionals selected by you or referred to you by us, because such individuals are outside our supervision and control.

ARCHITECTURAL AND ENGINEERING SEALS

Some cities and states are now requiring that a licensed architect or engineer review and "seal" a blueprint, or officially approve it, prior to construction due to concerns over energy costs, safety and other factors. Prior to application for a building permit or the start of actual construction, we strongly advise that you consult your local building official who can tell you if such a review is required.

ABOUT THE DESIGNS

The architects and designers whose work appears in this publication are among America's leading residential designers. Each plan was designed to meet the requirements of a nationally recognized model building code in effect at the time and place the plan was drawn. Because national building codes change from time to time, plans may not comply with any such code at the time they are sold to a customer. In addition, building officials may not accept these plans as final construction documents of record as the plans may need to be modified and additional drawings and details added to suit local conditions and requirements. We strongly advise that purchasers consult a licensed architect or engineer, and their local building official, before starting any construction related to these plans.

LOCAL BUILDING CODES AND ZONING REQUIREMENTS

At the time of creation, our plans are drawn to specifications published by the Building Officials and Code Administrators (BOCA) International, Inc.; the Southern Building Code Congress (SBCCI) International, Inc.; the International Conference of Building Officials (ICBO); or the Council of American Building Officials (CABO). Our plans are designed to meet or exceed national building standards. Because of the great differences in geography and climate throughout the United States and Canada, each state, county and municipality has its own building codes, zone requirements, ordinances and building regulations. Your plan may need to be modified to comply with local requirements regarding snow loads, energy codes, soil and seismic conditions and a wide range of other matters. In addition, you may need to obtain permits or inspections from local governments before and in the course of construction. Prior to using blueprints ordered from us, we strongly advise that you consult a licensed architect or engineer—and speak with your local building official—before applying for any permit or beginning construction. We authorize the use of our blueprints on the express condition that you strictly comply with all local building codes, zoning requirements and other applicable laws, regulations, ordinances and requirements. Notice: Plans for homes to be built in Nevada must be re-drawn by a Nevada-registered professional. Consult your building official for more information on this subject.

DISCLAIMER

The designers we work with have put substantial care and effort into the creation of their blueprints. However, because they cannot provide on-site consultation, supervision and control over actual construction, and because of the great variance in local building requirements, building practices and soil, seismic, weather and other conditions, WE CANNOT MAKE ANY WARRANTY, EXPRESS OR IMPLIED, WITH RESPECT TO THE CONTENT OR USE OF THE BLUEPRINTS, INCLUDING BUT NOT LIMITED TO ANY WARRANTY OF MERCHANTABILITY OR OF FITNESS FOR A PARTICULAR PURPOSE. **ITEMS, PRICES, TERMS AND CONDITIONS ARE SUBJECT TO CHANGE WITHOUT NOTICE. REPRODUCIBLE PLAN ORDERS MAY REQUIRE A CUSTOMER'S SIGNED RELEASE BEFORE SHIPPING.**

TERMS AND CONDITIONS

These designs are protected under the terms of United States Copyright Law and may not be copied or reproduced in any way, by any means, unless you have purchased Reproducibles which clearly indicate your right to copy or reproduce. We authorize the use of your chosen design as an aid in the construction of one single family home only. You may not use this design to build a second or multiple dwellings without purchasing another blueprint or blueprints or paying additional design fees.

HOW MANY BLUEPRINTS DO YOU NEED?

Although a standard building package may satisfy many states, cities and counties, some plans may require certain changes. For your convenience, we have developed a Reproducible plan which allows a local professional to modify and make up to 10 copies of your revised plan. As our plans are all copyright protected, with your purchase of the Reproducible, we will supply you with a Copyright release letter. The number of copies you may need: 1 for owner; 3 for builder; 2 for local building department and 1-3 sets for your mortgage lender.

TOLL FREE
1-800-521-6797

REGULAR OFFICE HOURS:
8:00 a.m.-10:00 p.m. EST, Monday-Friday,
10:00 a.m.-7:00 p.m. EST Sat & Sun.

If we receive your order by 3:00 p.m. EST, Monday-Friday, we'll process it and ship within **two business days**. When ordering please have your credit card or check information ready. We'll also ask you for the Order Form Key Number at the bottom of the order form.
By FAX: Copy the Order Form on the next page and send it on our FAX line: 1-800-224-6699 or 520-544-3086.

Canadian Customers
Order Toll Free 1-877-223-6389

ORDER TOLL FREE!
FOR INFORMATION ABOUT ANY OF OUR SERVICES OR TO ORDER CALL

1-800-521-6797
Browse our website:
www.eplans.com

BLUEPRINTS ARE NOT REFUNDABLE
EXCHANGES ONLY

FOR CUSTOMER SERVICE,
CALL TOLL FREE 1-888-690-1116.

HELPFUL BOOKS FROM HOME PLANNERS

1 BIGGEST & BEST

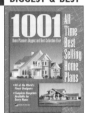

1001 of our Best-Selling Plans in One Volume. 1,074 to 7,275 square feet. 704 pgs. $12.95 1K1

2 ONE-STORY

450 designs for all lifestyles. 810 to 5,400 square feet. 448 pgs. $9.95 OS2

3 MORE ONE-STORY

475 Superb One-Level Plans from 800 to 5,000 square feet. 448 pgs. $9.95 MO2

4 TWO-STORY

450 Best-Selling Designs for 1½ and 2-stories. 448 pgs. $9.95 TS2

5 VACATION

430 designs for Recreation, Retirement, and Leisure. 448 pgs. $9.95 VS3

6 HILLSIDE

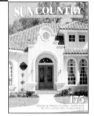

208 designs for Split-Levels, Bi-Levels, Multi-Levels, and Walkouts. 224 pgs. $9.95 HH

7 FARMHOUSE

300 fresh designs from Classic to Modern. 320 pgs. $10.95 FCP

8 COUNTRY HOUSES

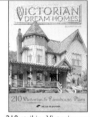

208 unique home plans that combine Traditional Style and Modern Livability. 224 pgs. $9.95 CN

9 BUDGET-SMART

200 Efficient Plans from 7 Top Designers, that you can really afford to build! 224 pgs. $8.95 BS

10 BARRIER-FREE

Over 1,700 products and 51 plans for Accessible Living. 128 pgs. $15.95 UH

11 ENCYCLOPEDIA

500 exceptional plans for all styles and budgets— The Best Book of its Kind! 528 pgs. $9.95 ENC3

12 SUN COUNTRY

175 Designs from Coastal Cottages to Stunning Southwesterns. 192 pgs. $9.95 SUN

13 AFFORDABLE

300 modest plans for savvy homebuyers. 256 pgs. $9.95 AH2

14 VICTORIAN

210 striking Victorian and Farmhouse designs from today's top designers. 224 pgs. $15.95 VDH2

15 ESTATE

Dream big! Eighteen designers showcase their biggest and best plans. 224 pgs. $16.95 EDH3

16 LUXURY

170 lavish designs, over 50% brand-new plans added to a most elegant collection. 192 pgs. $12.95 LD3

17 WILLIAM E. POOLE

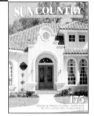

100 classic house plans from William E. Poole. 224 pgs. $17.95 WP2

18 HUGE SELECTION

650 home plans— from Cottages to Mansions 464 pgs. $8.95 650

19 SOUTHWEST

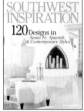

120 designs in Santa Fe, Spanish, and Contemporary Styles. 192 pgs. $14.95 SI

20 COUNTRY CLASSICS

130 Best-Selling Home Plans from Donald A. Gardner. 192 pgs. $17.95 DAG2

21 COTTAGES

245 Delightful retreats from 825 to 3,500 square feet. 256 pgs. $10.95 COOL

22 CONTEMPORARY

The most complete and imaginative collection of contemporary designs available. 256 pgs. $10.95 CM2

23 FRENCH COUNTRY

Live every day in the French countryside using these plans, landscapes and interiors. 192 pgs. $14.95 PN

24 SOUTHWESTERN

138 designs that capture the spirit of the Southwest. 144 pgs. $10.95 SW

25 SHINGLE-STYLE

155 home plans from Classic Colonials to Breezy Bungalows. 192 pgs. $12.95 SNG

26 NEIGHBORHOOD

170 designs with the feel of main street America. 192 pgs. $12.95 TND

27 CRAFTSMAN

170 Home plans in the Craftsman and Bungalow style. 192 pgs. $12.95 CC

28 GRAND VISTAS

200 Homes with a View. 224 pgs. $10.95 GV

29 MULTI-FAMILY

115 Duplex, Multiplex & Townhome Designs. 128 pgs. $17.95 MFH

30 WATERFRONT

200 designs perfect for your Waterside Wonderland. 208 pgs. $10.95 WF

Home Planners wants your building experience to be as pleasant and trouble-free as possible.
That's why we've expanded our library of do-it-yourself titles to help you along.

31 NATURAL LIGHT

223 Sunny home plans
for all regions.
240 pgs. $8.95 NA

32 NOSTALGIA

100 Time-Honored
designs updated with
today's features.
224 pgs. $14.95 NOS

33 DREAM HOMES

50 luxury home plans.
Over 300 illustrations.
256 pgs. $19.95 SOD2

34 NARROW-LOT

245 versatile designs
up to 50 feet wide.
256 pgs. $9.95 NL2

35 SMALL HOUSES

Innovative plans for
sensible lifestyles.
224 pgs. $8.95 SM2

36 OUTDOOR

74 easy-to-build designs,
lets you create and build
your own backyard oasis.
128 pgs. $9.95 YG2

37 GARAGES

145 exciting projects from
64 to 1,900 square feet.
160 pgs. $9.95 GG2

38 PLANNER

A Planner for Building or
Remodeling your Home.
318 pgs. $17.95 SCDH

39 HOME BUILDING

Everything you need to know
to work with contractors
and subcontractors.
212 pgs. $14.95 HBP

40 RURAL BUILDING

Everything you need to
know to build your
home in the country.
232 pgs. $14.95 BYC

41 VACATION HOMES

Your complete guide
to building your
vacation home.
224 pgs. $14.95 BYV

42 DECKS

A brand new collection
of 120 beautiful and
practical decks.
144 pgs. $9.95 DP2

43 GARDENS & MORE

225 gardens, landscapes,
decks and more to
enhance every home.
320 pgs. $19.95 GLP

44 EASY-CARE

41 special landscapes
designed for beauty and
low maintenance.
160 pgs. $14.95 ECL

45 BACKYARDS

40 designs focused solely on
creating your own specially
themed backyard oasis.
160 pgs. $14.95 BYL

46 BEDS & BORDERS
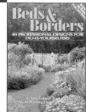
40 Professional designs
for do-it-yourselfers
160 pgs. $14.95 BB

BOOK ORDER FORM

YES! PLEASE SEND ME THE BOOKS I'VE INDICATED:

To order your books, just check the box of the book numbered below and complete the coupon. We will process your order and ship it from our office within two business days. Send coupon and check (in U.S. funds).

☐ 1:1K1 ....$12.95	☐ 17:WP2 ....$17.95	☐ 33:SOD2 ....$19.95
☐ 2:OS2 ....$9.95	☐ 18:650 ....$8.95	☐ 34:NL2 ....$9.95
☐ 3:MO2 ....$9.95	☐ 19:SI $14.95	☐ 35:SM2 ....$8.95
☐ 4:TS2 ....$9.95	☐ 20:DAG2 ....$17.95	☐ 36:YG2 ....$9.95
☐ 5:VS3 ....$9.95	☐ 21:COOL $10.95	☐ 37:GG2 ....$9.95
☐ 6:HH $9.95	☐ 22:CM2 ....$10.95	☐ 38:SCDH $17.95
☐ 7:FCP $10.95	☐ 23:PN $14.95	☐ 39:HBP $14.95
☐ 8:CN $9.95	☐ 24:SW $10.95	☐ 40:BYC $14.95
☐ 9:BS $8.95	☐ 25:SNG $12.95	☐ 41:BYV $14.95
☐ 10:UH $15.95	☐ 26:TND $12.95	☐ 42:DP2 ....$9.95
☐ 11:ENC3 ....$9.95	☐ 27:CC $12.95	☐ 43:GLP $19.95
☐ 12:SUN $9.95	☐ 28:GV $10.95	☐ 44:ECL $14.95
☐ 13:AH2 ....$9.95	☐ 29:MFH $17.95	☐ 45:BYL $14.95
☐ 14:VDH2 ....$15.95	☐ 30:WF $10.95	☐ 46:BB $14.95
☐ 15:EDH3 ....$16.95	☐ 31:NA $8.95	
☐ 16:LD3 ....$12.95	☐ 32:NOS $14.95	

Books Subtotal $ _____
ADD Postage and Handling (allow 4–6 weeks for delivery) $ 4.00
Sales Tax: (AZ & MI residents, add state and local sales tax.) $ _____
YOUR TOTAL (Subtotal, Postage/Handling, Tax) $ _____

YOUR ADDRESS (PLEASE PRINT)

Name _____

Street _____

City _____ State _____ Zip _____

Phone (_____) _____ — _____

YOUR PAYMENT

TeleCheck® Checks By Phone℠ available

Check one: ☐ Check ☐ Visa ☐ MasterCard ☐ American Express

Required credit card information:

Credit Card Number _____

Expiration Date (Month/Year) / _____

Signature Required _____

Home Planners, LLC
3275 W. Ina Road, Suite 220, Dept. BK, Tucson, AZ 85741

Canadian Customers Order Toll Free 1-877-223-6389

HPT95

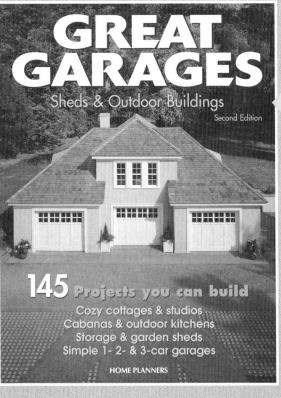